Courage to Change
The Freedom Movement

**The Fall of the Dark Players
Dismantling the 3D Grid,
& The Grand Rising of Humanity.**

Copyright© 2024 by Sherri Divband

Table of Contents

Part Three: The Dawn Of Freedom 196

Dedications

This book is dedicated to my family. I have so much love for you that it doesn't fit in my heart.

For my husband, Kas, you are my greatest love. You are my rock, my best friend, and my biggest supporter. You truly saved me from myself. You believed in me even when I didn't believe in myself. Without you, I would not be the person I am today.

For my son, Jordan, you will never know what you did for me and how you saved my life. Your light brought me back to life; I am eternally grateful. I am honored to be your mom and will always be by your side, no matter what. Never let this world dim your light. You are extraordinary.

For my son, Skyler, you are truly special. I have never met anyone with as big of a heart as you. Your thoughtfulness, curiosity, compassion, and wisdom have taught me so much. You have shown me what pure love feels like. Because of you, my perspective of the world has shifted, and I am eternally grateful.

For my daughter, Aramis, no words can describe how you have changed my life. I believe you are one of my greatest teachers. From the moment you were born, you changed everything. You have opened my eyes in ways I never dreamed of. I only hope to make you proud one day.

For my dad, Bill. I cherish your unconditional love and support. I am grateful that, no matter what, you are a positive light in my life. You have taught me to appreciate the little things in life, even during the darkest times.

For my second mom and dad, Simin and Khosrow, I don't know what I would do without you both. You have supported me in ways I never dreamed of, and my heart is filled with so much gratitude and love. Thank you for your unconditional support throughout the years; it has never gone unnoticed.

INTRODUCTION

This book is a continuation of my previous book, *Starseeds and The Great Awakening*. For the past decade, I have had the privilege of working with people all over the world to help mentor and guide them throughout their spiritual awakening. As an intuitive energy healer and spiritual coach, I facilitate communication between the soul of my clients as well as their guardians, guides, animal companions, angels, and star families. I have worked with babies in the womb, newborns, children, adolescents, adults, and the elderly. I have assisted souls coming through the birth portal by delivering important messages to their parents, as well as helping souls transition out of this life. I have spent many years communicating with a new wave of children coming to this planet to truly *innerstand* their path and why they have chosen to incarnate at this time.

I have assisted countless families to help them navigate through false labels such as Asperger's, ADHD, ADD, Autism, and Dyslexia. I have assisted many children in understanding their psychic abilities and how to integrate with 3D without becoming attached to it. I have worked with clients to help them discover their souls' origin and why they have chosen to come into this timeline. I have spoken to beings from parallel universes: Andromeda, Pleiades, Arcturus, Alpha Centauri, Orion, Sirius, Lyra, the Sun, Venus, Mars, and Inner Earth. I have connected with feline hybrids, deities, sasquatch, fairies, dragons, blue avians, angels, arch angels, animal spirits, indigenous hybrids, and other interdimensional species.

I learn something new every week as I continue to work with clients from all corners of the planet. I constantly receive new information and messages for my clients; however, it has become clear throughout the years that this information is meant to be shared with the collective. That was my intention for my previous book, and as I have gathered more information over the past year, I have more to share.

Courage to Change, the Freedom Movement, is very special to me. I have split this book up into three parts: 3D Influence, It's Time to Heal, and The Dawn of Freedom. In the first section, I have included more dark players' agendas, and manipulation tactics centered around psychological influence. In part two, I share powerful ways to begin the process of healing, igniting your innate abilities, and becoming spiritually centered. In part three, I share ways to progress as a collective and unite to break down the programming and dismantle the 3D grid.

The information included in this book is a compilation of my own experiences and information I have received while in my sessions, channeled messages, and the personal journeys of my clients. To preserve the privacy of my clients, I do not use their real names.

To shift the energy surrounding certain words in our vocabulary, I use the phrase innerstanding instead of understanding throughout this book. I use this word a lot because it is essential that in this transition period, we remember our power and recall the wisdom that comes from within us. As we transmute the dark programming, we birth new energy of strength and sovereignty. *Innerstanding* represents our innate power, intuition, and connection to the universe. As humanity rises, we will no longer be suppressed within the confines of *understanding*. The Grand Rising of humanity is about breaking free from control and embracing an era of infinite potential that aligns with the collective's highest good.

PART ONE

3D INFLUENCE

THE LION AND THE SHEEP

In my previous book, *Starseeds and the Great Awakening*, I spoke extensively about 3D interference. The dark players can manipulate humanity in countless ways through targeted attacks, directed energy weapons, and dark magic. Predictive programming and MK Ultra work through 3D influence and repetition. Children are targeted at a young age to mold their minds to influence their likes, dislikes, and overall belief systems through consistent and repetitive programming. For any negative program to work, it must first break the spirit, insert suggestions, and create a loop to follow.

Throughout my sessions with people over the past twelve years, I have seen a clear shift in the collective consciousness resulting from the fall of Atlantis, where a patriarchal leadership system became prominent, shifting the trajectory of humanity into the 3D. If we look back through humanity's past in linear time, much evidence supports this. During the time of Lemuria, as well as in various indigenous tribes throughout the planet, there was an affinity towards the divine feminine as the creators, the manifestors, the mothers, and the leaders of society had a direct connection to their ancestors. The people of these societies worked cohesively to maintain balance and connection between one another. Over time, due to masculine influence, things shifted, and their leaders carried forward an agenda for ultimate control. Humanity began to shift into survival mode and succumbed to control through generations of programming.

I believe that due to an instinct to survive, humans as a species tend to have a herd mentality. They want to feel like they belong to something significant. Most people enjoy being around others and crave human contact, meaningful relationships, and love. There are natural leaders, and there are natural followers. These two contrasting personality traits create societies that thrive with give & take and collaboration. Some people do not feel comfortable leading, whereas others excel at it. If everyone were in charge, nothing would get done. Individuals must be willing to step back and follow the guidance of others. The leaders are the architects of ideas, structure, and solutions. The followers can put their egos aside to maintain structure and bring balance to their community. The leaders can guide with humility and compassion. In an ideal society, everyone plays their role, and both groups work together harmoniously. There is no right or wrong; it is simply part of the human experience.

Due to this natural dynamic of human behavior, the dark players have used that against us to create a controlled network of corrupt leaders and a society of blind followers. This is popularly known as the *sheep vs. lion* mentality. The lions historically have been the leaders, whether those people are our parents, teachers, law enforcement, elected leaders of society, or self-proclaimed leaders. Nonetheless, they influence humanity in some way, whether on a large scale or not. Regardless of their intentions, the sheep follow.

The sheep are people that the lions easily influence. The sheep will mindlessly follow the masses for many reasons. One reason is that they have submissive personality traits. They prefer to be guided and directed because it's easier to follow than to develop their ideas. They may be unsure of their abilities. They might be shy and reserved, so they would not cause trouble. They may have imprinted fears from their parents, which prevent them from taking risks or going against perceived rules or boundaries. From my experience working with people of all ages in many countries, I have noticed that most sheep have low self-esteem and low self-worth. This can be for a variety of reasons, most likely childhood traumas, lack of love, lack of support, addiction, abuse, indoctrination, and exposure to 3D interference.

For a control matrix to thrive, *sheep* are the preferred quality in a human being. They will mindlessly follow the mainstream rules without question. In my previous book, *Starseeds and the Great Awakening*, I explained how children reach a pivotal point around age five and six, where they anchor into their human bodies. Out of survival instinct, they begin to succumb to their parents' will, and what they perceive as *normal* behavior, and as a result, they become less multidimensional. In essence, they become more *3D*. The school system is designed to capture children during a vulnerable period of human growth through repetitive conditioning, indoctrination, and memorization. These are simply distractions set forth by the dark players to begin the process of dimming their light. Through years of undivided attention throughout grade school, children slowly lose their sense of individuality and imagination as they begin to blend like *sheeple*.

The structure of the 3D is designed in a manner where the majority of the population follows the rules and guidelines. Societal expectations passed down from generations lead people to believe there is a normal process of being a productive member of society. Children go to school, get good grades, compete with other children for limited opportunities, and memorize and regurgitate information. They begin to blend in with one another, leading them to lose the life spark that makes them unique and different. Unfortunately, this leads to young adults who shy away from being distinct from others and seek ways to blend in. Many people are pressured into university level education for more indoctrination and preparation to go into the work force, becoming slaves to large corporations so that the dark players become rich and powerful. All the while, most adults are unhappy, unfulfilled, and depressed because they are spending their lives doing a job rather than following a passion. Much like sheep confined to one pasture, they exist, not thriving.

Many Starseeds are the lions of today. They are the leaders, the way showers, the rule-breakers, and the pioneers of change. They are not afraid to stand out or to be different. They prefer to be unique and don't care what others think. Lions don't do well with authority figures and often rebel against rules and authoritative figures. In my sessions, I have seen an increase in evolved beings that have volunteered to come to the Earth's third dimension to assist in awakening humanity and helping people break out of the loop of control.

As I shared in my previous book, these ascended beings come from all over the cosmos, descending in frequency to be in a human form. Many of these beings spend 100s of Earth years in preparation for their role in this life. Many are used to being in a light body, so adjusting to a dense body is challenging. Many of these beings come from pure love and are not used to being in a toxic reality bombarded with common frequencies such as shame, fear, and guilt. Integrating as a human is challenging and not without side-effects. As we continue through a grand awakening, more and more lions will emerge from hibernation, and they will shift the trajectory of controlled leadership. They are future leaders who will be humble, motivational, and compassionate and lead with dignity and grace.

WHY INCARNATE AS HUMAN?

I have been told that incarnating as a human in the third density of consciousness within the third dimension of Earth is one of the most challenging places a soul can go. This merits the obvious question: *why incarnate as a human? Is there a way that souls can assist us from the astral plane and not inhabit a human body?* These were serious questions I had throughout the years as I embarked on my spiritual journey. It wasn't until I began having sessions with clients of all ages and backgrounds that I started to get answers a little bit at a time. Over the past twelve years, I have had the honor of working with exceptional people who are within very powerful soul groups. I have learned many things that have contributed to my innerstanding of one of my most significant questions. It opened my eyes to the possibility of multiple answers to the same question, which led me to believe that we may never truly grasp the whole picture in human form. However, we can certainly expand our minds beyond the limitations of 3D to have the freedom to tap into the collective consciousness of infinite knowledge.

It has been explained to me that the reason souls choose to incarnate as humans is because the body is a necessary component of the 3D grid system. In order for the soul to anchor their light to the planet, they need a body to serve as a vessel or a conduit to bring the light through. This is a vital part of the integration process, where a higher bandwidth of light creates a channel between the soul and the planet. The body is the access point. The soul's expansive light merges with the body, and that light vibrates out to shift the frequency of the third-dimensional grid. When there are massive amounts of Starseeds in human form, they harmonize and send out a powerful frequency that works to break down the firmament or the barrier that keeps the grid intact.

I was once shown the metaphor of a cardboard box to represent Starseeds' impact on 3D over many generations. Imagine a basic cardboard box that represents the 3D. The box is taped up on all sides, and no light is coming through because all the cracks are sealed. The seal is made up of inorganic energy that creates a film around the box to keep the box's integrity solid and impenetrable to outside elements. Some call this sealant the firmament, a barrier anchoring souls inside. The 4th dimension is accessible to 4th density beings, such as demons and dark entities, who can easily travel between 3D and 4D. The firmament is a highly advanced technology that always keeps the vibration low. This is enhanced by weather modification, satellite technology, 3G, 4G, and 5G towers, underground and above-ground portals, EMFs, and various other mechanisms.

Because of this intricate network of fail-safes to keep people under the illusion of free will, it has been difficult for spirit guides, galactic beings, angels, and other beings to assist humans in the past. That is why ascended beings have tried in the past to incarnate as humans to assist humanity in an awakening. These ascended beings have never been able to succeed in their mission because not enough of humanity was ready to awaken. It's as if the box was sealed so tight that people felt safe within it. Like an abusive child, they would rather stay with their abusive parents because that is all they know, and on some level, they feel safe. The uncertainty of the world outside their home makes them unwilling to seek help. Similarly, humanity has been trapped within an illusionary box of captivity for so long that people have become adjusted and complacent, even comforted by the trauma.

Over the past hundred years, more and more ascended beings of light have chosen to incarnate within this box because there is power in numbers. As each light being is incarnated within the box, it's as if they pass through the birth portal, leaving a tiny pinhole through the boundary of the box. Over time, there are millions of little holes, and as more come, the frequency rises, which means their light is more robust. The stronger the light, the larger the hole. I see the Starseeds of the modern day coming through like comets of light into our atmosphere, and while doing so, they break down the firmament more and more. In 2024, I am shown that the box formally representing the 3D has lost its shape and integrity. There are so many holes that the light breaks down the grid at exponential speeds. The box is collapsing, so souls that have previously been fast asleep wake up. At record speeds, more and more people are waking up every day. I believe the momentum we have made in this era is because so many beautiful souls chose to incarnate as humans, to be on the battlefield, and to fight a spiritual war for the sovereignty of many lost souls, which has an impact on many other universes.

PSYCHOPATHS & SOCIOPATHS

Within the 3D, many archetypes, or split personalities, stem from fragmented souls. The 3D thrives on low vibrational emotions, traumas, and dis-ease of the collective. There are two common archetypes known as psychopaths and sociopaths that are among the most fractured souls. I believe a soul incarnates with a destiny, or a blueprint, of their life plan. They come in with a generalized theme, lessons to learn, a healing journey, or a life of service to guide others. Some can come with all the above and are the most advanced souls. The tricky part about incarnating as a human is that you forget the blueprints once you go through the birth portal. At least, this has been the case for centuries. Upon birth, a soul is bombarded with 3D interference, 3D influences, programming, implants, and negative entity influence.

A soul can begin fragmenting at a young age due to the continuous bombardment of various negative frequency bands, indoctrination, trauma, and societal expectations. Fragmenting means that the soul's light begins to dim, and the light can fractal into segments or compartments stored within the conscious mind. This will split the person's personality, and depending on the environment, one or more personality traits will become dominant. That is why children who suffer from repeated trauma from a young age go into *fight-or-flight* mode, where they are in survival mode most of the time. Their dominant personality trait becomes the survivor, and they do things they must do to survive. They are less empathetic towards others because they have developed an *everyman-for-themselves* mentality. Unfortunately, this is the story for many.

A dominant archetype is the psychopath. Over the years, I have developed my library of characteristics that I have seen in a psychopathic, fragmented soul. First, it appears that they have lost connection to their soul at some point. It's as if their soul dissociated so frequently throughout their life that one or many entities moved into the open space of consciousness. The person has lost their way, leaving room for the shadow side to dominate. They have no sense of boundaries, convictions, or moral compass. They become pathological liars because the compartmentalized personalities within them are not in harmony with each other; therefore, they live within many truths. They don't even know they are lying because they do not control their thoughts, words, and actions.

Not only do they self-sabotage, but they sabotage the people in their lives. They create chaos and feed off the energy of the drama. They can be aggressive and have psychotic episodes where they black out because another entity takes control of their body. This is when psychopaths become violent and physical towards others. They have dark fantasies and often act them out in real life. They prey on innocent people and feel pleasure when they dominate others. They are likely to have addictions to drugs, sex, and alcohol. I believe psychopaths are trapped within the darkness of their minds. Their soul is lost and no longer in control.

A sociopath is another archetype like a psychopath; however, they are more misguided than dissociated. They are still connected to their soul, yet they heavily influence the 3D energy around them. They are often misguided by their entourage of negative entities. They are heavily affected by 3D influence and interference, whereas the psychopath has succumbed to it. Sociopaths may not treat others with kindness, and they can be hurtful in their actions, but they do feel remorse. Their empathy is still present, and they are less tuned in to it than a soul that hasn't endured as much trauma. Sociopaths get their validation in unhealthy ways. They are likely driven by power, money, and material things. They are narcissistic and sloppy liars. Psychopaths will lie with a straight face, whereas a sociopath forgets their lies, get confused, and are more likely to get caught. The difference is that they don't care and will push their lie as it suits them instead of admitting they are wrong. They lack boundaries, compassion, and respect towards others. In many cases, sociopaths don't have a positive role model while growing up to show them what positive and balanced relationships look like. Conversely, they are abused, neglected, and unloved; therefore, the foundation of their reality is built upon abuse, neglect, and lack of love.

Both psychopaths and sociopaths are narcissistic, self-centered, and not in touch with reality. Unfortunately, many of them have endured abuse and trauma throughout their life, which contributed to their dissociation. Without a solid foundation of love and support during the most vital periods of development, it is easy to become lost within the 3D paradigm. Once a soul loses its way, it is more likely to become tethered to 3D. It is easier for entities to take over their vessel, and the soul can lose control indefinitely.

TOXIC SHOCK

It was explained to me during a session many years ago with a child who struggled with non-stop health issues from birth that the 3D was causing her toxic shock. It immediately made me think of Toxic Shock Syndrome (TSS) women get from the use of tampons. TSS is a life-threatening complication of a bacterial infection that can also be from open wounds. The symptoms can range from fever, dizziness, fatigue, diarrhea, vomiting, rashes, headache, and, more severely, organ failure. Coincidentally, these are similar symptoms that Starseed children experience, especially during their earlier years in development. This is because they are bringing in so much light, and their body must acclimate to a higher density than their body is used to. Our DNA has been altered throughout generations, and our genetics have shifted. In the epigenetics section, I spoke about this extensively in my previous book, *Starseeds and The Great Awakening.*

Because many Starseeds are born with more advanced *Spiritual DNA*, the dormant human DNA is activated. This is causing a massive shift in psychic abilities and heightened senses. Conversely, this is putting more strain on the body. More and more children are experiencing seizures, developmental delays, and extreme sensitivity to the environment. I believe the reason children are experiencing an energetic *toxic shock* is because they are profoundly shifting their human DNA. However, while humanity is still connected to 3D during this transition period, their environment is toxic compared to their consciousness. It would be like oil and vinegar, trying to mix as one liquid solution. No matter how much you stir them together, they will not thoroughly mix. It's as if they co-exist in the same space. Still, they can't come together in a homogenous capacity.

Today's Children are the oil trying to mix with the vinegar of programming. They are not conforming like the previous generations, causing a beautiful transition in consciousness. Many of the Starseeds children of today are kind, loving beings who are showing us how to be leaders and followers in a more evolved and spirited way. Today's children are shifting human physiology with their light. The toxicity of the 3D is evident, and these children are slowly activating the human body to absorb more light and activate dormant DNA. I have been told repeatedly through my sessions since 2023 that this is an adjustment period. There will be a breakthrough for the children having the most challenging time acclimating to their bodies. This breakthrough won't manifest in the way you might be thinking. The setbacks and their willingness to struggle now create the tides of change.

This is an uncomfortable period in our evolution that only the most advanced souls signed up for. As more and more light enters the 3D matrix, it shifts the planet's balance. New frequencies are assisting with grid work, terraforming the opening of portals, and activating dormant DNA. The toxic shock will catalyze and awaken the masses. As more people awaken, more light comes through until the 3D grid breaks down. Once the structure and foundation of the 3D grid have fallen, humanity's Grand Rising will occur, and we can continue to pass through the 4th density of healing and continued transition into 5D. It is my innerstanding that 5D is only a marker point of freedom; however, the possibilities are endless from that point on. We are not limited to 5D, but we will exist in 5D as our new foundation where Starseeds can live in bodies without limitation; therefore, toxic shock will no longer exist.

THE VOID

The void has been brought up in countless sessions over the years. The best way to describe the void is a space between the dimensions. Typically, souls travel between dimensions relatively smoothly if they are at a density that resonates with each transitionary frequency. However, suppose there is confusion, fragmentation, or manipulation of a soul in transition. In that case, it can become trapped in a space between. I refer to this space as the void because that is the term I have heard in numerous sessions. The void has come up in so many of my client sessions because it is one of the energetic holding spaces through which lost souls are reincarnated. A network of entities, extraterrestrials, and human hybrid bloodlines has controlled the third dimension. I referred to this group as the dark players in my previous book.

The void was created to trap souls now of death as they transition from a physical body back to their oversoul. This is also referred to as their consciousness. When a human dies, their soul leaves and is reunited with their own light source. A soul can have many incarnations simultaneously; however, they have one primary source of light, which is their consciousness. Their consciousness holds their spiritual blueprint, akashic records, and the wisdom of their collective incarnations. There is a beautiful process of sovereignty and freedom to choose when and where a soul decides to incarnate.

A soul can choose a very challenging life to learn valuable lessons. A soul can also choose a life of exploration on an entirely new planet of their choosing to expand their soul's experience. There is no limit to the soul's journey and where they can go if the journey matches their density of consciousness.

The soul trap cycle is often referred to as the wheel of samsara or the negative wheel of reincarnation. Through my sessions, I have learned that there are many ways a soul can become trapped within a negative cycle. The most common is when a person dies in a traumatic way through murder, suicide, or a tragic accident. The sudden death causes confusion at the moment of death, making them vulnerable to becoming trapped in the void. Dissociation is another way a soul can be tricked into following a false light. A dissociative death through dementia, psychosis, and the soul choosing to separate from the body in the final moments of life can all contribute to a soul becoming lost once it crosses over.

From what I have been told when a soul leaves the body, a beautiful bright or golden light gently guides them back to their oversoul, pure light. They can be greeted by galactic beings within their soul group as well as Earth-bound spirits to ensure they find their way home. A false light created by the dark players using technology creates an inorganic white light. This white light has a powerful magnetic pull tuned to a low frequency. When a soul dies in a traumatic way, they are in a low frequency as they leave their body. As a result of this low frequency, they can be pulled into the strong vortex of energy created by the false light, which then takes them through a tunnel of light and into the void. Many people see this tunnel of light during near-death experiences. It has been depicted similarly throughout non-fictional books, interviews, and movies.

Through my sessions, I can see visions, receive downloads, hear sounds, and telepathically communicate with galactic beings, angels, Earth spirits, and my client's higher self. In many sessions, when I learned about the void, I could see it through my client's perspective, who was once trapped within it. It appeared dark, cold, and noisy. There were terrifying sounds of people crying out for help. Shamans often refer to this space as the underworld. I was guided to the underworld with the assistance of a shaman many years ago. From what I recall, it felt very similar to how the void was shown to me. It was dark, there were a lot of lower vibrational entities, and it was a very desolate and ominous environment. There was the risk of becoming trapped in the underworld if you didn't know how to protect yourself. At that moment, I was guided to see duality: consciousness's positive and negative aspects. It was a powerful experience to see the darkness of the underworld. However, I never had any interest in going back!

Once the soul is trapped in the void, it becomes fragmented, and that aspect of the soul becomes disconnected from its oversoul. The fragmented consciousness can't be separated from the oversoul; however, the signal is so faint it is difficult for the two parts to communicate. The souls that are within the void are reincarnated for many lifetimes. The lives generally have a negative theme that fuels the 3D grid with loosh. This lower vibrational energy feeds dark entities. The loosh keeps the grid thriving like gasoline keeps a car going. Lives of enslavement, disease, poverty, trafficking, addiction, suppression, and fear are among the common themes. Through technology and heavy fragmentation, the soul is anchored to the void through a powerful magnetic pull that gives the illusion they are trapped. As a soul is inserted in a cycle of negative lives, many of which end in suicide, murder, or trauma, the illusion becomes stronger. It's as if they become tethered or anchored to the void, which makes it difficult to get out.

BREAKING FREE OF THE VOID

The first time I heard of souls being rescued from the void was during a child's session in 2022. In that session, I was told this boy was part of a group of souls that rescued lost souls from the void. I remember thinking how crazy this sounded, considering this soul was just a 12-year-old child. He showed me that during sleep time, or when he was in a theta state of relaxation while playing video games, he could astrally travel into the void. I thought this was interesting, considering how many children I work with play video games. Could they do similar work in the astral while *plugged* into their game? I was told that many children who zone out while watching TV or playing video games can occupy their conscious minds while their souls are out doing other things.

There are multiple layers to what we can see in 3D. Depending on your density, your perception shifts, and you can tune into more than someone limited to a lower density. There is a dark side, a light side, and everything in between. In this case, video games serve many roles. For the dark players' agenda, they can sabotage a child's innocence by inserting violence and negative programming into the games they are playing. Subliminal messaging and different forms of MK Ultra can be embedded into the games. Playing frequent games can disconnect them from the real world, creating an escape for them to hide and be something they are not. Video games keep children indoors, which disconnects them from nature and bombards them with EMFs. Video games have become the modern playground where children play with their friends in a virtual world and do not socialize face-to-face as much as previous generations. These are all examples of the negative impact gaming has on children and adults. However, if we expand our perception and look from a different lens, we can see a positive benefit emerge.

There are a lot of advanced souls incarnated as children at this time, and many of these souls come from planets with technology that is far more advanced than ours. I have been told repeatedly by Starseed children that they are bored here on Earth. Some choose to pass the time when they appear zoned out while watching TV or daydreaming, to travel astrally. They do this to get out of their bodies so they are free to entertain other areas of their consciousness. They can also astrally travel during sleep time, just like adults. Some travel to the void to rescue lost souls. Some travel to stargates to activate and protect the integrity of the portals. Some of them travel to their home planet to continue learning. Some visit their councils to discuss what they are going to do next. There are many places they can go, depending on what they are here to do in this life.

Think about a cat, for example. They sleep for up to 18 hours a day. Where do they go when they sleep? I have been shown that they travel astrally so they can be free from the limitations of their body during those periods. Pets, in general, can travel astrally while they sleep and go to many places. I have been told that one of their favorite things is to be with their human companion, so they go to work or school with them. They protect and support their family members throughout their day, even if their human companions can't see them. Of course, it's not feasible for humans to sleep all day like cats, so humans must find other ways to relax deeply enough to astrally travel safely. Meditation, video games, watching TV, and listening to music are ways to escape reality and tap into a higher level of consciousness where astral travel is possible.

Rescuing souls from the void is an operation that has been going on for thousands of years; however, it is my understanding that it accelerated in the late 1990s to the early 2000s. There is a large group of Earth Angels incarnated as humans at this time who are rescuing lost souls and doing humanitarian work in their human lives to protect children. I have a lot of adult clients in this soul group. These angelic souls have been guardian angels to many children in the past, some of which were taken into the void. Countless souls are trapped in the void connected to a human incarnated in this life. To take it further, some souls have a fragmented aspect of their soul trapped within the void, so they send another fractal as a human in this timeline to rescue themselves.

The more I learn about the void, the more complicated it becomes. The most important thing to take away from all of this is to innerstand that such a place within the quantum field exists. It is ruled by advanced galactic and Earth beings and is run by artificial intelligence. The good news is that the void is breaking down, and the false light tunnel can no longer pull souls within it. There are many reasons why the negative wheel of samsara is breaking down, and I will do my best to explain it throughout this book.

IS THE EARTH FLAT?

There are a lot of misconceptions within the collective on the firmament and whether we are on a flat Earth. The flat Earth ideology has been circulating for quite some time; however, it didn't become a popular topic of conversation until the COVID-19 pandemic. Many awakenings occurred during that period, triggered by many layers of deceit. I believe it was during that period that the lion archons within the collective began to wake up. When people started to question everything, they had ample time to research while the world was in lock-down. Research led many people down a *rabbit hole*, where one question led to another and another until they were so far down the hole they emerged into a whole new world.

Because a mass awakening is not conducive to the control parameters of the dark players, they had to insert lies within the truther community to offset the leaked truths. The flat Earth theory was one of those lies that spread throughout the truther community like wildfire. It caused much friction, and even the brightest of lions became misguided. Mass confusion was the agenda used by the dark players to cause division once again within the group of people trying to gain access to the truth. The infiltration of the game *"Two Truths - One Lie"* became real life. It was a strategic tactic to cause uncertainty within the newly awakened community, causing frustration that led to many debates and divisions. The distraction stirred the pot of loosh that the dark players fed on for years.

It is my innerstanding, based on the thousands of sessions I have had over the years, that Earth can be flat, round, toroidal, and purely energetic depending on the level of consciousness the soul is connecting to. For example, a soul trapped within 3D for hundreds of years will be programmed so profoundly that they might connect to the concept of a flat Earth. The more you connect to the box, the more comfortable you are within it. The more you thrive within the box, the more it becomes part of you. You and the box become one. When that occurs, your reality becomes much smaller, and barriers are preventing you from expanding in consciousness. Unknowingly, many people consent to the limitations of the box. The firmament becomes a dome around you, trapping you within its energy field. Suddenly, you have no access to other dimensions as they are beyond the barriers of the box. In essence, you are within a grid, a two-dimensional plane with a limited network of experiences controlled by a greater power. I believe that is the flat Earth, which is authentic to those connected. It has become their home, their shrine, and they will go to any length to protect it.

For those souls that come to break down the box, their perception of Earth can look very different. Earth can appear round or a toroidal field of continuously moving energy. There are no limitations to how we can perceive our reality. Our density of consciousness is what gives us the ability to shift and expand what we visualize and experience. I believe most people who are open and not fully connected to the box of 3D live within a spherical planet. The most common perception is a round Earth with many dimensional fields within its three-dimensional plane. A round planet gives the freedom of expansion through a multidimensional reality. The boundaries are less rigid, and the illusion fades. This is why many Starseeds can connect to higher levels of consciousness while operating from a 3D body. Some people have an easier time tapping into their innate gifts, while the 3D illusion still blocks others. There is a mix of consciousness, densities, and perceptions within a round Earth. However, within the 3D box, people are seemingly disconnected from anything outside their limited boundaries of consciousness.

As souls connect to higher levels of consciousness, their reality expands. This creates a toroidal field, a magnetic field comprising many frequencies. Indigenous Earth spirits and beings connected to the Inner Earth exist within a toroidal field. A toroidal field of energy is ever-changing. Matter shifts in a higher frequency and becomes fluid and interchangeable. Manifestation becomes instant with infinite potential. I can see humans breaking free of the 3D box within the next ten years, connecting to a round Earth and evolving into a fourth-dimensional toroidal Earth with the ability to be just light. Once humanity escapes from the captivity of the box, they genuinely have the free will to experience whatever their soul desires.

SELLING YOUR SOUL

The concept of selling one's soul is a false narrative driven by dark programming and manipulation. To sell your soul would mean that a soul is, in fact, for sale. Throughout my years of one-on-ones with clients, I have been repeatedly told that a soul can't be sold because that would give rights and ownership to another soul, which goes against the laws of the universe. All fractals of God are sovereign and have free will to explore the many universes within the quantum. The collective wisdom and experiences throughout the network of infinite conscious beings are recorded within the Akashic records, which all souls can access. Because of the vast amount of information stored within the Akashic records, guardians are in place to protect its integrity. Because all souls are sovereign, they can choose to remain in the light for the highest good of the collective souls, or they can choose to break off into the abyss of the unknown to be within the darkness.

I believe that, regardless of whether a soul chooses the light or turns their back on God, they are still a delicate part of the collective of infinite souls. Much like a parent who has a troubled child who has been imprisoned for murder and may have hurt them deeply, there is still a part of them that is connected to that child. I feel God would not turn away from lost souls because they are, in fact, lost. Energy is energy, and souls are energy that have a consciousness. This soul signature separates them from trillions of other lights within the cosmos. Within our infinite network of universes are planets with war, destruction, and power struggles that exist alongside planets of peace and love. If a soul has endured more traumatic incarnations and their soul is severely fragmented, they are vulnerable to succumbing to the dark light. When a soul is wounded within their spiritual blueprint, they are more tempted by darker, more powerful souls that feed off the energy of power.

When a soul is energized by overpowering the will of another soul, there is a darkness within them that grows. This darkness attracts other dark souls and energy fragments that are not actual souls. These fragments are like shadow beings without consciousness, just negative energy fragments existing in the ether. When a soul becomes powerful enough to take hostage of a soul that was tricked into giving away its sovereignty, it technically owns that soul. It's a type of contract where a soul willingly agrees to be controlled by the more powerful entity in exchange for protection or some other arrangement. When a soul gains the consent of many souls, they now have established an army of dark souls to run the halls of the universe like a bully and his minions in a schoolyard. This network can start wars, fight other dark, powerful groups, and gain control of even bigger armies of darkness.

This is when the enslavement of souls can happen, and the boundaries of free will are broken. The rules are bent, and souls are manipulated into *selling their souls* to be a part of something they believe is to their benefit. I am told through many client sessions that this usually doesn't end well for the soul that willingly joins a dark force because, ultimately, they are betrayed and become slaves to the dark players controlling the group. The collective can both idolize and fear the dark players throughout the cosmos. The dark nature of their consciousness is never fully content with their power, and they often crave more. It's as if they are trying to fill a void that can never be filled because it's a black hole that goes on for eternity. That is how the darkness works - it pulls you in until you realize there is no way out. At least, that is what they want you to believe.

Within the 3D box are many dark players made up of a network of cosmic beings: reptilians, Draco's, grays, hybrids, and powerful entities with no form. There are AI lords with armies of beings that follow a hive mind. A network of demons, dark entities, Jinn, and low vibrational beings also prey upon humans. Whether for food, enjoyment, rituals, sacrifices, loosh or to control the 3D reality, they have their hierarchies and minions to keep the 3D thriving.

The notion of selling one's soul has surfaced in the past decade. It's a dark agenda being pushed through multiple outlets within the 3D. The entertainment industry is at the top, with heavy influence on celebrities to sell their soul to be part of the Illuminati or the dark players' insider club. Whether celebrities are in music, television, movies, modeling, fashion, or reality TV, they must join their club to be superstars. Essentially, they are selling their soul by signing a contract and performing one of many rituals. The ritual performed is to summon a dark being that will be connected to that celebrity moving forward. That dark being will take over the celebrity's body at certain times, which creates two versions of the person, and sometimes more if there is more than one being connected to them.

Once the celebrity is initiated, they begin their campaign to influence as many people as possible. The dark players use celebrities like an army of influencers tasked with hijacking the minds of the youth and the vulnerable. Music, movies, television, fashion, and social media are utilized as their playground to lure innocent people in so they can continue the programming process. Celebrities use various methods to encourage young minds to be open to selling their souls because that's how they became famous. They sing about it in their Billboard top hits. They brag about it in interviews. They wear satanic attire with devil horns and upside-down crosses. It's common to see musical artists on stage with portals in the background using witchcraft to summon demons.

Concerts have become loosh arenas where dark beings are released through these portals to feed off the excitement and energy of the crowd. Unknowingly, children are singing along to songs that have spells intertwined in the lyrics with subliminal messaging. It has become mainstream to chant and call upon dark spirits during concerts, and most people attending think it's for entertainment, not realizing that they are the ones entertaining the dark entities as their energy is being harvested.

More movies and series are coming out every year that have themes of witchcraft, superpowers, the underworld, and other dark themes to desensitize our youth. This leads to more curiosity and the potential to experiment with dark energy. Without training and the knowledge of how to protect themselves, people are at risk of entity attachments. When someone experiments with dark energy, they often open energy portals without realizing it. This invites entities from the 4th dimension to come through. As more and more portals are opening, the darker beings are coming through. With many low-vibration beings running loose throughout the 3D, the more negative influence there is on humanity. Those who are struggling with addiction, depression, illness, sadness, anxiety, and a sense of belonging become targeted by entities that will encourage them to remain in a dark space, preventing them from healing. This is another level of 3D influence that stems from celebrities, influencers, and the elite glamorizing a dark narrative.

Throughout all the programming, many children are losing their way and inadvertently selling their souls by consenting to the agendas inserted within the collective. As I explained previously, no one can actually sell their soul, but what ends up happening is that they consent to renting their consciousness in this life to entities that will control and manipulate them if they are under the spell of *fitting in* or participating in the negative agendas. As people continue to listen to artists in the dark club, go to their concerts, watch their movies, and buy their clothing or make-up lines, they will attract the entities attached to that artist.

I recognize how difficult it is to avoid artists and movie stars not in the club since such a high percentage exists. With social media and a plethora of streaming platforms, our lives are bombarded with suggestive programming daily. It's almost impossible to avoid listening to certain artists when restaurants, shopping centers, TikTok videos, television shows, and movies are playing their music. Instead of hiding from it, I coach my children and many clients not to consent to the negative programming within the song or movie. For example, my daughter likes the artist, Drake. I don't know Drake, nor can I say whether he is in the club or not. Therefore, I encourage her to practice the same affirmation before listening to *any* artist, regardless of whether they have publicly announced that they have sold their soul.

The intention we set while watching a movie or singing along to the lyrics of a song is essential. If we don't put any intention, then we are susceptible to subliminal messaging and spell casting simply by singing the song. The dark players believe that if you listen to the music, buy the albums, watch the shows, wear clothes with dark symbolism, and idolize their celebrities, then you have consented to their dark agenda. It's a back door entrance to giving consent without you having to say that you are giving consent verbally. Knowing this, I encourage my children to say they don't consent to anything not of their highest good while listening to the artist. They don't have to say anything out loud. While listening to music, they can say, *"I do not consent to any 3D interference or influence from this artist that does not align with my highest good, and so it is."*

The same goes for scary movies. I don't watch horror movies, and I encourage people to avoid them; however, since there are so many out there, I can see how people are attracted to watching them. What people don't realize is that while watching a scary movie and a person becomes frightened, they activate the black box technology. In my book, *Starseeds and The Great Awakening*, I explained black box technology, so I will not go into detail here. I will say that TVs, computers, tablets, and smartphones are portals, and they can be activated by different things, such as sex magic, fear, sadness, and shame. Laughter is one emotion that does not activate the portal because it is a high-vibrational emotion. Some entities will be attracted when the portal is activated by one of the lower vibrational emotions. They will come through the portal to feed off the loosh given off by the person or people watching the movie. Horror films and pornography are two sure ways to activate the portal and invite negative beings through.

Whether a person is listening to music, watching a film, or wearing make-up and clothing by designers, it is beneficial to get into the habit of not consenting daily to anything and everything that is not serving your highest good. That way, you don't have to drive yourself crazy trying to figure out if a particular celebrity has sold their soul or not. No one knows for sure who is in the club. Many will speculate and have compelling evidence, but at the end of the day, no one knows for sure. So, instead of trying to get a definitive answer, it is more empowering to get in the habit of not consenting to a broad spectrum of 3D influence daily so that you don't inadvertently attract dark spirits to your energy field that may influence your behavior and ultimately attempt to take control of your consciousness.

THE LEFT BRAIN

The left-brain mentality of 3D is an agenda brought forth by the dark players. When a society is hyper left-brain centered, they are easier to manipulate and program. That is because when a person is perpetually operating from a highly logical and objective mindset, they are more likely to disconnect from their spirit. Loops are created through repetitive patterns, which are reinforced by left-brain thinking. Throughout generations of left-brain training, humanity has lacked the ability to be subjective and intuitive. So much of our reality is based on procedures, facts, equations, research, and scientific evidence. Thus, metaphysical and esoteric studies have become *woo-woo* and discounted because no scientific studies validate the integrity of what cannot be seen.

The mainstream public schools have adopted a highly left-brained curriculum, heavily discounting imagination, emotional, adventurous, and creative studies. There is a lack of grassroots education where children learn the foundations of agriculture, homesteading, basic trades, mindful math principles, fundamental sciences, connection with nature and animals, and creative and emotional intelligence. The standard day curriculum is based on memorization and regurgitation, heavily influencing technology. We are already seeing evidence of the current generation being disconnected from nature. At the same time, they are tethered to technology, smartphones, video games, and social programming.

I believe the right brain is not being utilized as it should be. As I have stated many times, everything is about balance and moderation.

Society should be taught a mixture of technology, spiritual and fundamental science, and basic foundational life and survivor skills. The children of today need balance. They will learn how to integrate the left and right brain through balance for optimal health, wellness, intelligence, and overall well-being. There is a reason we have two hemispheres of the brain, and excluding one side from the other is not serving our highest good. We need the primal aspect of our brain just as much as the creative. When both hemispheres work together, we have the potential to operate at our best. When the collective is operating at its best, it benefits us all.

Below are some examples of Left and Right Brain processes and activities. I recommend taking a moment to assess which areas you are more dominant and which areas require more practice. You don't need to resonate with everything. The ideal space to be is slightly dominant on one side yet in resonance with the other.

Left Brain (YANG)	Right Brain (YIN)
Logical	Creative
Ego	Intuitive
Analytical	Imaginative
Linear	Multidimensional
Verbal	Telepathic
Rational	Emotional
Cautious	Adventurous
Objective	Subjective
Impulse	Regulation
Repetition	Fluid

Left Brain (YANG)	Right Brain (YIN)
Micro	Macro
Computer coding	Arts and crafts
Math	Creative writing
Engineering	Gardening and grounding
Problem-solving	Music

ANXIETY IS A 3D VIRUS

Just as inflammation is the underlying physical effect of dis-ease in the body, anxiety is the underlying effect of 3D influence and interference on humanity. I believe anxiety is a virus embedded within the program of the matrix. Anxiety is the binding agent between fear and the detachment of our souls from our bodies. If you think about anxiety from a logical perspective, it is a physiological response to an imminent threat. The symptoms of anxiety include sweating, uneasiness, irregular heartbeat, headache, panic attacks, body tension, erratic behavior, depression, arousal, negative thoughts, butterflies in the tummy, and more. Now, let's analyze why our body reacts that way. What energy induces those physiological responses? Where does anxiety come from?

The human body is phenomenal. There are so many mechanisms of checks and balances to ensure a homeostatic environment. When something is off or there is a perceived threat, the body will either compensate or alert the brain that there is danger. Similar to a *fight-or-flight* situation, the brain processes this threat, and the physiological response is to flee, fight, or freeze. In the case of anxiety, the body can't pinpoint the danger, so the body doesn't know how to prepare for the impending attack. That's why people experience a myriad of symptoms. The body is trying to tell the brain that something is not right. The cause may be idiopathic or unknown; nevertheless, the body's alarm bells are ringing.

According to Mental Health America, anxiety disorders are the highest reported mental health issue in the US, with 42.5 million

Americans claiming to suffer from this illness. NIH reports that 31.1% of adults in the US experience anxiety at some point in their lives, and the statistics for children are increasing every year. In my opinion, from working with thousands of clients, many of whom suffer from some level of anxiety, our body is trying to get our attention. Anxiety is an essential piece of the puzzle for the collective. Our souls are trying to send us an *SOS*. Our souls are trying to speak to us in a language we will understand. Heart palpitations, tension in the body, insomnia, and restlessness can be a blatant nudge to break us out of our slumber.

The dark players can connect us to the matrix through varying degrees of fear, manipulation, and programming. In that case, anxiety is our higher self attempting to tell us that what we are experiencing is not for our highest good. I believe anxiety is valid and often debilitating. Unfortunately, big pharma's solution is pumping us with mind-numbing medication to keep us subdued enough so that we resist the temptation to go within to see what is going on. Empaths have the most challenging time because they feel everyone else's anxiety like alarm bells ringing off the hook. If they are not trained to release it, they can take it on as their own. I believe the collective needs to take a long and severe look at anxiety, and perhaps we can agree that it represents a call for help.

PART TWO

IT'S TIME TO HEAL

My intention for writing this section of the book is to share the most common anchors to 3D. When anyone embarks on a healing journey, there will inevitably be setbacks. It's human nature and part of our programming to stop when things get difficult, because healing can be a painful process. The pain I am referring to is emotional, mental, and physical. As we begin to peel back the layers of trauma, there is no telling what we will find. Sometimes, it can be so challenging that we often put the brakes on healing and revert to what we know and what's comfortable, our worst habits and crutches. In the past, I have been there, and I still occasionally make a pit stop there from time to time. Self-love is one of the most humbling experiences. I will share throughout this section the most common roadblocks I have seen in my clients and myself.

My hope is that while reading these common setbacks, you will find the strength within yourself to persevere through any block that comes your way, even if it's you. I have coached a lot of teens to *fuel the fire within them.* What I mean by that is to take the anger, frustration, rage, fear, resentment, limiting emotions and *ignite them*. Channel that energy towards something powerful. I encourage you to fuel the fire within yourself and channel it towards the healing techniques I will share in the coming chapters. It's time to reclaim your wellness and truly heal.

I have chosen what I feel to be the simplest ways to release, transmute, protect, process, and heal on a soul level. There are also many other ways to heal. I offer you what I have done for my own healing, what I have done for clients, and what I have taught for many years. I provide easy techniques that I feel anyone can do, so long as they believe in themselves. Feel free to take what resonates with you, and don't be intimidated to try them all at least once. If one technique doesn't work for you, that's ok. Just don't make the mistake of discounting the rest. A big part of the process is finding what resonates. It can be many different things or just a few. Once you find the ones that work best, you will feel like you have a foundation of techniques to work with, giving you a sense of empowerment. Remember to take one day at a time. Healing is a marathon, not a sprint.

CONFRONTING OUR SHADOW SIDE

I have spoken about the shadow side in all of my books because it is extremely important that we do not fear it. The shadow side lives within the Ego and feeds off our consciousness's darker aspects. The shadow side is the wounded aspect of us that has endured hurt, betrayal, fear, rage, jealousy, envy, and loss. As that energy seeps deep within the subconscious, it is either learned from, buried, or amplified. When a person experiences deep trauma, an aspect of their light dims. Sometimes, the experience can be too painful to process, so the soul dissociates from the experience and becomes buried in the subconscious. The only issue is that it can resurface at the least desirable time. If a soul experiences trauma and becomes taken over by the trauma through bitterness, rage, and resentment, this can activate their shadow side. They become a darker version of themselves. People with an active shadow side seek revenge. They become hyper-critical, pessimistic and tend to attract other people who are in the same vibration. As I mentioned earlier, most sociopaths and psychopaths begin with a trauma that is not healed. Over time, they close off their light, and their shadow side takes over.

Negative thoughts seep deep into the subconscious when the shadow side is in control. Then 3D influence and interference can grab hold of you, and you become a prisoner to your own warden. Despite karma, curses, hexes, negative energy cords, and spells, I believe we all embody the power to break free from our own imprisonment. We often create these prisons in our minds with our own negative thoughts. Then, the dark ones will send their minion parasites to feed off the negative energy. After reviewing countless past lives of my clients, I have noticed that, over time, our shadow sides have become more prominent. As a result, I feel as though we must work twice as hard to keep it under control. Although our reality is built upon inverted truths and false illusions, unfortunately, to some degree, we have created the reality many of us are so desperate to escape.

On some level, we need to reflect and take responsibility for the role we have played or contributed to the collective loop of suffering. Personally, I take responsibility for the dark period that I went through in my teens and early twenties. I succumbed to the darkness, and my shadow side grew exponentially. My bitterness and resentment blinded my judgement, and instead of taking responsibility for my actions, I blamed everyone else. I feel as though a lot of people who have endured any level of trauma tend to project their anger when in reality it is a loss of control they are feeling. When someone steals our power, our primal instinct is to lash out to protect ourselves. Some even seek revenge, and until that void is filled, they insert themselves in a loop of continued trauma.

As we grow in our conscious awareness, we often reflect and recognize the role we played during certain events from our past. We may even feel shame or regret. I believe it is that shame and regret that ignites our shadow side even further. When I coach clients who experience shame for the way they behaved during specific periods in their past, I always tell them to release it. Why hold on to it? We certainly can't go back in time and change it. Instead, we can be grateful for the lesson learned and move on. We can check that box of *lessons learned* and try our best not to repeat it.

I think souls volunteer to experience this density of consciousness in order to experience contrast. A big part of this contrast is to experience the emotions that go along with the experience. The shadow side plays a significant role in the experience of contrast. The darkest depths of our thoughts and our most troubled desires are in contrast with our greatest strengths and accomplishments; however, there is a spectrum of frequencies in between. I think we are meant to experience all facets of the spectrum that are in alignment with our highest good. That doesn't mean we are taking the easy road; it just means that the hardship we endure is teaching us something of value.

The problem I see, which seems to be our biggest downfall, is the extreme nature of contrast perpetuated by 3D interference that brings us out of balance and out of alignment with our soul. I believe that when humanity gains control of our freedom, we will embark on an evolutionary path that will be conducive to a reality consistent with duality, if that is what we choose. The main difference will be that it will enhance our growth as a species, not limit us.

BREAKING OUT OF THE LOOP

In my book, *Divinely Guided*, I explained how easily children can get stuck energetically in repetitive patterns. It's human nature to find comfort in routines, regardless of whether or not they are healthy for us. The repetition can create a pattern of energy that is cyclical. For example, waking up in the morning, taking a shower, getting dressed, having breakfast, going to work, coming home, having dinner, watching TV, and going to bed, day after day, is a routine. The physical body, the mental body, and the emotional body get used to this pattern, and it almost becomes second nature. There is a specific dynamic of energy that creates a loop or a cycle.

From many years of working with clients of all ages, I have noticed that people find themselves in different types of loops throughout their lives, both negative and positive. There can be loops of bad relationships, trauma, illness, and hardship. There can also be loops of happiness, windfalls, and great success. Due to the bombardment of 3D influence and negative programming, it is much easier to get trapped within a negative loop indefinitely. Many clients come to me feeling blocked and unsure of how to shift their life out of survival mode. I work with a lot of clients who have a history of narcissistic relationships that occur one after the other, like a revolving door of abusive partners. I believe that people get trapped in energy patterns that generate experiences that match the vibration of their loop.

If a person breaks free from an abusive partner yet lacks the confidence and ability to reflect on the experience and truly heal, they will attract another abusive partner. This is a loop of abusive relationships that will continue until the person believes they deserve more because they are worthy. One of the biggest challenges people have is their desire to be loved. When they lack love for themselves that they are trying to attract, it can cause a block. There are so many negative affirmations that are broadcasted to the collective through Voice of God technology, which I spoke about in my book, *Starseeds and The Great Awakening*. A common 3D interference tactic is the persistent shame program that is injected into our reality through body shaming, judgement, low self-confidence, competition, and gluttony. The dark players are able to accomplish this in many ways, such as TV and movie programming, fashion, celebrities, influencers, social media, and imprinted societal standards. The question people should be asking themselves is, who sets these standards? Who decides what type of fashion is in style? Who decides what is sold at the food markets? Who decides what shows are on mainstream platforms? Who decides what is in and what is not? Who decides what our children are learning in school? Who sets the standards of health and wellness?

Most people reading this book innerstand that a complex network of influential players has controlled the 3D grid for centuries; however, that reign of control is breaking down. More and more people are waking up and asking the right questions. People are demanding more because they are stepping out of their own loops of repetitive programming. Once you break free from the loops, you begin to see things more objectively. Within a loop, you are the experiencer. There are emotions at play as well as vulnerabilities to 3D influence. It's almost like being in a hypnotic trance. The longer you are in a loop, the less you realize you are within one. This makes it more challenging to recognize the warning signs that you are trapped within a negative 3D cycle. When you are able to exit out of a loop, it is much easier to recognize the signs, which is where the phrase *hindsight is 20/20* comes from.

Negative Loop Red Flags

Here are some common red flags to help you determine
if you are in a negative loop.

***You consistently attract friends and/or partners who don't value
you or your self-worth.**

***You consistently attract romantic partners that verbally, mentally,
or physically abuse you.**

***You have anxiety about change even if you know it would be
beneficial for you.**

*You are consistently taken advantage of throughout your life.

*You consistently find yourself in the middle of drama.

*You consistently feel lost and hopeless.

*You consistently feel like no one understands you.

*You consistently experience hardship.

***You feel uncomfortable when your life seems peaceful, and you
are often waiting for something terrible to happen.**

This is a small list of examples to give you an idea of how we can become trapped and not realize it. Most people wouldn't even suspect they are in an energetic pattern because it has become a *normal* part of their lives. Much like riding a wave in the ocean, you don't feel in control as you are at the mercy of the current.

Breaking Free

Breaking free from loops takes time and patience. It's really a choice once you recognize that you are in a loop. It's all about shifting your mindset. Our thoughts are so powerful that they can literally facilitate a physiological response within the body. Anxiety is an example of this. Suppose someone has anxiety about leaving their house because they are sensitive and overstimulated by the outside world. In that case, going out can put their body in a *fight-or-flight* response. Their sympathetic mode will activate, and their body will release cortisol and adrenaline due to a perceived threat. They may start sweating, their heart rate will increase, and they can become paralyzed with fear. In this scenario, if the person goes into *fight-or-flight* daily at the thought of leaving the house, which triggers a panic attack, sweating, and the release of stress hormones, resulting in their inability to leave their home. Now a loop has been created.

The best way to break free from a loop is first to recognize that you are in one. The first and most important step is recognizing the patterns. I tell my clients to write down the main aspects of the loop they have identified, such as addiction, abusive relationships, financial insecurities, and dis-ease. Then, write down the identifiable patterns that often appear cyclical when laid out. There may be more than one loop; however, I suggest working through one loop at a time. The body can only process and heal so much at one time. I recommend going easy and allowing time for the release and integration to occur, which can look different for everyone. Once you identify a loop, it's time to begin the process of unraveling the layers to facilitate the healing process. I will list my favorite methods to break free of patterns and what has worked for myself and my clients.

The Triggers

Writing down the triggers is essential in helping you identify what is anchoring you to the loop. To the best of your ability, write down as many things as you can think of that trigger you within the loop you are in. For example, if you are working through alcohol addiction, a trigger can be when you are around friends who drink. Another trigger can be when you see people drinking in movies. Another trigger can be when you eat a particular type of food that pairs with your favorite drink, such as margaritas and tacos, red wine and steak, or brunch and Bellini's. You get the idea. The objective here is to try your best to write down as many triggers as you can think of.

Progressive Breathing and Release

The next thing I recommend is to create a new pattern of repetitive release work that you incorporate into your daily routine. This doesn't cost any money, and it is my personal favorite method to release trapped emotions, fear, negative energy, and 3D anchors. In this case, you release energy connecting you to any triggers or patterns. I do this type of breathing exercise multiple times a day. Doing this regularly makes me feel a difference in my mental clarity, peace of mind, and overall well-being. Progressive breathing can be the most effective way to shift your autonomic nervous system from sympathetic mode to parasympathetic mode. I will share with you my own combination of visualization, intention, and breathwork into one powerful exercise.

Progressive breathing

1. In your mind or out loud say, "I bring to the surface any and all energy, cellular memory, and trapped emotions that are no longer serving my highest good." Visualize all that dense negative energy pulling from your feet, hands, limbs, abdomen, head, chest, and organs and pulling into your lungs. Visualize a color as it all comes to the surface of your awareness.

2. Take a nice big breath for the count of 4, breathing in through your nose and into the belly. Feel your belly expanding outward.

3. Hold your breath for the count of 6 while visualizing all you are releasing is within your lungs as the color you have identified— for example, brown dense energy.

4. In your mind, say to yourself, "I choose to release it now." And with a nice long exhale through your nose for the count of 8, let it go.

5. Visualize the brown dense energy leaving your body as you exhale, transmuting into light as it merges with the atmosphere around you.

6. Follow this process for one to two minutes or until you feel your body relax. With each breath you will feel your shoulders relax, your heart rate slow down, and your overall energy shift to a more balanced state.

This process works even better when you do it in nature, as you can ground simultaneously as you release. Once you are finished, feel yourself anchored into the Earth. Visualize your feet growing energetic roots deep within the Earth to ground and rejuvenate you. You can enhance the process with crystals, soft music, and tuning forks.

Please note that the breath counts are suggested only. The power of this breathing technique is not the breath counts but rather the progressive nature of the breathing. The most important thing is to take a nice belly breath, hold that breath for a little longer than it took to breathe in, and exhale for longer than you held it. This is a controlled network of inhales, holds, and exhales. If you find it challenging to breathe in a 4-6-8 format, you can start with a 3-5-7 format or even a 2-4-6 format. Whatever works for you is right for you. The worst thing you can do is overthink this exercise and receive no benefit because you think you are doing it wrong. There is no wrong way to do this exercise. I am simply providing my favorite recipe.

Grounding

Once you have established a regular routine of progressive breathing, you will want to couple that with a grounding routine. I have covered grounding in all my books, so I will list my favorite methods here. I want to clarify that there are two intentions behind grounding that people may not consider. First, you are taking the time to connect to the planet, nature, and/or animals. This helps your body relax, rejuvenate, heal, and raise in frequency.

Grounding with Nature

- Going out in the sun

- Going to any body of water, such as a lake, river, waterfall, or ocean

- Salt baths. These are best done with Celtic or Himalayan salt (or a salt foot bath)

- Walking or running in nature

- Spending time with pets or wildlife

- Meditation with nature sounds or outside in nature

Second, grounding also means that you are connecting through the right brain to stimulate creativity and imagination to enhance the pineal gland.

Grounding with the Right Brain

- Arts, crafts, painting, and drawing

- Creating music, writing song lyrics

- Creative writing and poetry

- Automatic writing or psychography

- Sewing or designing clothes

- Cooking and creating recipes

- Using esoteric tools such as tarot, pendulums, tuning forks, and crystals

Heart Brain Coherence

Heart to brain coherence is a state of harmony between the two main aspects of human physiology. The human brain is an operating system that utilizes the senses, such as sight, sound, touch, and taste, to help distinguish what is happening in the world around it. The brain then processes those signals to instruct the body to regulate body temperature, release hormones, tense up, relax, and more. The brain doesn't experience anything; instead, it perceives experiences through our emotions and our senses and responds accordingly. The brain uses logic to access situations that are absent of emotion. Our brain is responsible for learning, attention, judgment, and holding back emotions to make clear decisions.

Our hearts contain neurites, are similar to the neurons in the brain. Our hearts radiate an electromagnetic field that can expand five to six feet outwards. Even research suggests that various emotions can create different heart patterns that can affect us in different ways. From a spiritual perspective, this can be seen through the auric field as a convergence of mind, body, and spirit. The heart is the aspect of us where emotions flow, intuition is the strongest, and we can generate profound connections with other people. At the same time, dominance in the left or right brain might be a common occurrence, when it comes to brain and heart coherence; the more balanced the brain is, the better.

Brain and heart coherence occurs when the brain and heart work together efficiently. This is established when the heart's electrical activity is in sync with the brainwaves. This can be represented within the autonomic nervous system (ANS), the body's regulatory system of the heart, blood pressure, hormones, brain rhythms, and digestive system. When the sympathetic nervous system (SNS) is activated, the body goes into a *fight-or-flight* response. The body shifts into survival mode when this occurs, secreting adrenaline, cortisol, catecholamines, and norepinephrine. The body prepares to defend itself from an impending physical, mental, or energetic attack. The body tenses up, and blood is shunted to the most vital organs: the brain, the heart, and the lungs.

When the body is triggered to relax, the parasympathetic nervous system (PNS) kicks in, which releases acetylcholine to lower the heart rate. Breathing begins to regulate, and the digestive system is activated. During this wave of relaxation, the body can release dopamine, endorphins, and/or melatonin. The emotions of peace, tranquility, and happiness can occur during this transition.

So why is the ANS so important for heart-brain coherence? Personally, I believe it is the physiological pathway for the mind, body, and spirit to work together. Scientifically, it can be proven that it is the process of integrating the body's regulatory system of cognitive function, physiological function, and emotions, which can be seen through both the ANS and the PNS. In other words, the heart and brain are in harmony. This powerful concept links two aspects of our DNA: primal cognitive function and spiritual and intuitive innate response.

I believe optimal communication with the heart and brain is paramount in enhancing our spiritual and physical evolution. We are less likely to become entangled within loops when both function optimally. We can, therefore, break free of 3D influence and limitations. The best way to enhance this connection is by mindfully exercising both hemispheres of the brain, the logical and problem-solving left brain, with the intuitive, imaginative, and expansive right brain.

Creating New Pathways

The last and most powerful step is to generate new pathways by making different choices. It can have a lasting impact, even if it's one small step in another direction. Going back to the example of alcohol addiction, let's say that person decides to skip out on an evening of partying with old drinking buddies. Instead, she decides to go out with a new co-worker to the movies or a social event with others who don't drink. She's now created a new pathway with new potential and new opportunities. The changes don't have to be big, and she doesn't have to leave all her old friends behind. She may have to put herself first for a while and choose to be around people who bring out a better version of herself without the temptations of triggering activities.

Repetitive cycles can create a physiological pattern with subsequent hormonal responses. Earlier, I used the example of the person in a loop who was afraid to go outside. In that example, the person created a physiological response within their body when they thought about going outside. An increase in cortisol, sweating, and an elevated heart rate resulted from them walking towards the door. The loop eventually created replications within the neurons in the brain to create a repetitive pattern, thereby facilitating a repetitive physiological response. It's almost like Groundhog's Day, where you could do your morning routine with your eyes closed before work. Within a cycle, our body literally gets used to a pattern, which almost becomes second nature.

Creating new pathways stimulates new neural networks within the brain so that the cycle stops and new connections are made. Being mindful of the smaller choices becomes pivotal in shifting the trajectory of your mind and body, making way for your spirit to lead. Again, there don't have to be significant changes. It's quite the contrary, where minor shifts tend to have a more substantial impact overall. Let's say that you are struggling with social media addiction. Every night, when you get home, your routine is to make dinner, feed the animals, clean the dishes, and plop on the couch with your smartphone to surf your social media feed.

A simple adjustment to the routine can shift the energy of the cycle. Perhaps, when you get home, you make dinner, feed the animals, and then walk. Instead of looking at social media when you return, you listen to an uplifting podcast or take a salt bath. If you have children, you take them out to the park. Whatever you do, you resist the routine and put your phone to the side. Maybe at the end of the night, you allot yourself 20 minutes on your phone, and you set a timer to ensure you don't go over the time limit. Before bed, you watch a funny show, read a few chapters of a book, play a card game with your children, or do a 15-minute guided meditation before bed. Whatever you choose, you are mindfully choosing to fill the time with activities that nourish your soul instead of limiting yourself to the repetitive pattern of social media.

It's certainly not easy to get out of a loop. Sometimes, the loop becomes so comfortable that the thought of leaving it can cause the SNS to activate, which generates cortisol and anxiety. Fear of change can be debilitating. The good news is that fear is a left-brained construct, and if you can shift into the right brain, the PNS is activated. The infinite possibilities of stepping out of the loop become apparent. Take your time with this process and be patient with yourself. Setbacks can occur, but roadblocks often steer you in a more optimal direction. Identifying the loops you are in is a powerful first step; however, true empowerment comes from the willingness to change.

NO ONE IS LOOKING AT YOU THE WAY YOU LOOK AT YOURSELF

One of the topics I speak about the most in wellness workshops is our relationship with ourselves. Throughout my years as an intuitive healer, I have learned much about the human experience and how the ego plays a significant role in everything we do and how we think. The ego is connected to the primal aspect of the human species. The ego has a direct link to the conscious and logical mind. In my first book, *Intuitive Transformation Evolution*, I referred to the ego and the conscious mind as our nemesis. Our ego can block our intuition and our ability to trust in our knowing, which is why I call it the nemesis in our life; it can cause us to second guess everything. The nemesis brings doubt when there doesn't need to be. We can create blocks when we overthink too much, causing our minds to swirl in negative thoughts and *what-if* scenarios.

The nemesis can also create fractals of our human consciousness, which, in turn, creates archons and limiting beliefs. The ego can take control and cause a person to compare themselves to everyone else, whether it be their success, appearance, personality, or many other attributes they feel they are lacking. This can lead to an unhealthy expectation of themselves and a constant battle to achieve a certain level of validation from others. They don't realize that the validation they seek is a void they created that only they can fill. When they look in the mirror, they are not happy. When they achieve their goals, they struggle to be proud of themselves. When they experience triumphs, they reflect on ways they could have done even more.

Aside from the ego and impossible standards set forth by the conscious mind, another factor plays a role in this. Our environment plays a significant role in how we feel about ourselves. As children, we look to the outside world for validation from our parents, other family members, and from those in our lives. When we don't feel protected, supported, and loved as a child, we lack the validation we need in order to thrive. The confirmation we receive in our earliest years allows us to learn, adapt, and grow. When we think we are on the right track, we gain confidence and a solid foundation where we feel we can do more. However, suppose we don't receive that critical support. In that case, we lose trust, we recluse, and begin comparing ourselves to others in a way that is not healthy. We start creating thought forms and patterns. For example, if we become more like our sibling, who gets the attention we don't get, then perhaps our parents will love us more.

Our irrational thoughts create a rocky foundation that sets the tone for the future. These repetitive patterns are how loops are made, from our ego, 3D influence, and lack of confidence that keeps us trapped within them. Throughout our collective ancestral history, it is my observation that, over time, it has become human nature to judge ourselves more harshly than the world around us. The expected milestones and bars of achievements we set for ourselves are too high. I believe that is because we are constantly seeking validation from traumatic periods in our childhood to the present. Suppose those periods in our past are not healed. In that case, they can become potholes in our timeline, which can draw negative energy within the holes, and collectively, they can block us in many ways. The good news is that we can begin the healing process once we become aware that we are our biggest block.

You are not for Everyone

To truly evolve, we must ensure that we operate from a place of balance and creative expression, which separates us from one another. Other people will either like the energy you put out and enjoy being in your presence, or they won't. It's about accepting that you are unique and can't make everyone like you. This would be an impossible task that would drain you of your true essence should you choose to embark upon it. Do not mold yourself into what others want you to be. Strive towards accepting and loving yourself the way that you are. It is from that place that true peace will follow. As you walk in your true path, fully vibrant and in a state of complete self-acceptance, those who match your frequency and align with what you represent and stand for will come into your life for the right reasons and at the right time. Those people will be your beacon of support to help you gravitate toward the direction you are already headed. They will ground and lift you when needed, and you will do the same for them. Cherish yourself. Accept and love who you are. Allow those who don't appreciate you to continue searching until they find their match and tribe.

YOU ARE YOUR BIGGEST BLOCK

Over the years, I have had so many profound breakthroughs with my clients. Through their healing, I feel I am healing along with them. It is a beautiful and synchronistic process because we can connect the dots as my client is shown why they are blocked and how their current life and past life experiences contribute to these blocks. From there, they can heal profoundly. When everything comes together, and it all makes sense, the logical brain can jump on board, bringing balance between the left and right brain, and that is where the magic happens.

Throughout thousands of sessions over the decade +, I have noticed a clear trend in my clients' inability to heal, find happiness, and find purpose in their lives. The main culprits are clients trapped in a loop, 3D programming, and self-sabotage. A combination of 3D influence, 3D interference, and trauma can all play a role. However, we need to identify the root cause to take it further. The root cause is a human's innate longing to belong. There is a strong desire for humans to feel significant and part of something bigger than themselves. That is why souls choose to incarnate as a predominantly social and interactive species. Successful societies are built upon collaboration and networking, and humans are innately natural unless programmed differently. However, there is a dualistic nature to the human design, including innate wisdom, lack of wisdom, likes, dislikes, strengths, and weaknesses.

When a soul integrates with a human body, they are exposed to certain elements, like the ego and emotions, that can make the experience more challenging. The *old souls*, or those that have lived many lives as humans, have adapted to the ego and emotions. It's clear when you come across those people because they seem to have it all figured out. They have a keen awareness and a high level of common sense. They may not be wealthy or successful to societal standards; however, they are content with where they are, regardless of what anyone thinks. Whether they received the validation they needed as a child or not, their life experiences have collectively given them a solid foundation. Those people are mostly relatively healthy and balanced and tend to lead others.

Another large percentage of the population has either endured many traumas throughout their lifetimes or has been trapped within the negative wheel of Samsara. When a soul endures a lot of traumas, mind control, programming, and disempowerment, their soul becomes fragmented. Over many lifetimes, their soul can split into many fragmented pieces. This can lead to a separation from the oversoul, and those fragments can become anchored to the density that they are in. There is a cellular memory of traumas built into the spiritual blueprint of the person, which can cause negative patterns. Not feeling good enough or unworthy of joy and happiness is a common virus running through the collective blueprint.

Suppose a soul is in a vibration of lack with low self-esteem. In that case, they are more susceptible to programming, negative loops, and self-inflicted blocks. I have seen it repeatedly where a client is desperate to find a loving partner to share their life with, yet they don't honestly believe they deserve it. They don't feel love towards themselves, so they are looking for validation in someone else. They inadvertently attract abusive partners that put them down and make them feel worse about themselves. What they don't realize is the universe is going to keep bringing those types of people into their lives until they realize that the abusive partnership they have is with themselves. Their nemesis controls them, likely attracting negative entities that feed off their energy, much like parasites.

Whatever the reason for our limiting beliefs, our negative self-talk, and our blocks, I have seen breakthroughs countless times. Once a person has the innerstanding that they are likely the root cause of their blocks, they have the potential to look at their life differently. They can begin to decipher through a process of reflection, asking, "Were there any patterns? Have I learned what I need to learn?" and more importantly, "Am I ready to move on?" Believe it or not, many would rather stay in a low vibration where it is comfortable and familiar than move into unknown territories. Once a person is ready to embark on the path of sovereignty, they must be prepared to experience and feel all necessary to shift and re-align to a higher frequency. The first step is accepting their role in all aspects of their life and how, at times, they may have resisted, bargained, and even pleaded with themselves not to lean into the lesson because it was too painful. Once a person releases judgement of themselves and surrenders to the healing experience, they may be surprised by the abundance of support and love they will receive from the universe.

THE POWER OF SURRENDERING

I have learned that surrendering is one of the most profound healing methods. I believe our human survival instincts place us in survival mode, especially within the box of 3D. When people are in the sympathetic mode of *fight-or-flight*, they feel like they are constantly moving against the stream. It's like being on defense the whole game while your opponent is strategizing and in a place of offense. In the game of life here on Earth, the opponents are the 3D dark players who work together to control the matrix. Once humanity recognizes that we are playing a game that can't be won, the illusion will break down, and the realization that exiting the game altogether is the winning move.

I am not referring to exiting the matrix through death. I am referring to the collective awakening and the breakdown of the box we have been confined to and then anchoring to a higher dimensional plane of existence. We do this by centering ourselves to tune into the spiritual battle that has been taking place. Once people innerstand why the box was created and why the dark players want to steal the souls of millions of people, perhaps we can move to a place of offense and shift our strategy.

Disconnecting from our ego and reconnecting with our higher self will transcend all spells, manipulation, and programming. Only then can we pull in more life force energy, open our pineal gland, expand our intuition, tap into our innate knowing, and connect with the collective consciousness. First, we must start with the process of surrendering. I can almost guarantee that anyone reading this book has reached a point in their journey where they are ready to step into their power. Perhaps you are trying to figure out how to start or continue. Either way, I encourage those of you reading this to make a mental list of all the aspects of your life that you have tried to control, even if you got sick because of resistance to change, even if you lost friendships because you were too stubborn to take responsibility for your role in the drama, even if you burned bridges. After all, you were unwilling to give up control, even if it didn't serve your highest good.

We have all experienced some degree of resistance, stubbornness, and absolute unwillingness to shift our point of view throughout our lives, whether emotions, lack of inner reflection, or low self-esteem were the culprits. I have learned in my sessions, as well as throughout my healing, that the most powerful way to release blockages is by surrendering to them. When you shift out of defensive mode and shift into a neutral space, you can take a pause. Then, you can ask yourself, *"What is this experience trying to teach me? Am I resisting the lesson by standing in my way? Am I ready to surrender?"* Once we stop fighting a lesson, we move from survival mode to a vibration of critical thinking without extreme emotional influence.

Letting go releases an incredible amount of energy trapped within the body. When there is an abundance of trapped emotions, such as anxiety, fear, resentment, and guilt within the body, it can manifest physical illness. Everything begins as an energetic experience manifesting in our reality's physical element through touch, smell, vision, and sound. Our body will respond to experiences based on our emotional reactions. If we feel fearful during an experience, we begin to feel uneasy, which triggers a physiological response of adrenaline, cortisol, muscle tension, increased heart rate, elevated blood pressure, perspiration, and rapid breathing. Conversely, suppose we experience a situation of joy, we may smile and laugh, which produces endorphins, dopamine, and a feeling of relaxation and peace.

There are many ways to surrender. The fundamental process of surrendering is about letting go of control, taking a step back, and looking at your life as the observer. During a session I had many years ago, a client's spirit guide showed us a profound exercise in observing one's life. She explained that we don't need to die to review our lives. This concept comes from the theory that once we transition, we are given a life review to see how we handled the lessons we signed up for and if we accomplished what we set out to do in our life mission. Over the years, I have learned that succeeding is an ambiguous notion, and all life experiences are valuable because they add to our catalog of overall lessons and ever-expanding knowledge. All failures, successes, catastrophes, and triumphs get funneled into the collective consciousness, from which we can all benefit. Wisdom is a collection of energetic pathways and stories gathered throughout the cosmos. It's all information that translates to life, evolution, and creation.

Throughout the following few chapters, I will share with you my favorite ways to surrender, release, and facilitate the process of profound spiritual healing. An infinite number of modalities and techniques teach grounding and how to reconnect to the soul. I will share what has worked for me and how I have helped my clients. Having the courage to surrender is a big step in your journey. Stepping into a rhythm while you find the strategies that work for you is a critical step in the freedom movement. Without active participation from those within the collective who are ready for change, I believe humanity would remain in the 3D box for generations to come. As we stand together and regain our power, we become spiritually centered. Every day, more souls awaken, and one of the first questions I am asked is, *"How can I connect with my soul and exercise my sovereignty?"* I always tell them, *"If you are asking the question, you are farther than you think!"*

IT'S TIME TO HEAL

Every one of us is equipped with the innate knowledge to heal ourselves. It is imprinted in our genetic blueprint. We carry that knowledge throughout our lives as it is embedded in our soul's consciousness. Through my one-on-one sessions with clients, I have been told countless times that being human is one of the most challenging journeys. This is because of our spectrum of emotions and our drive to belong to something greater than ourselves.

In my first book, *Intuitive Transformation Evolution*, I discussed the importance of innerstanding our emotions and how they affect our wellness. The fundamentals of healing are the ability to go deep within the layers of programming until you find your true sense of self. How do we do that if we are bombarded with 3D interference and suggestive programming from the moment of birth? Our parents try their best to guide us; however, they are working through the lens of their programming. Our teachers try their best to guide us, yet they are limited to a core set of principles and curricula that the dark players approve of. Humans are influenced by parents, mentors, teachers, elders, friends, romantic partners, and those in power throughout their lives. Furthermore, humans must navigate those influences through their emotional spectrum. If a person doesn't know how to work with their emotions, their emotions can take control of them in their weakest moments.

When I was in a session with a client a few years ago, a beautiful guide told me that we must stop looking at holistic health as an alternative and instead return to our roots where primary care was holistic healing. Indigenous cultures have always believed in utilizing the Earth's plants as medicine for the body and the energy of Mother Earth to heal our souls. They understood the mind-body-spirit connection and how energy leads to good health and happiness.

EMOTIONS

Our emotions are one of the most influential aspects of our human experience. All emotions have an energetic frequency or resonance. Humans experience life through their emotional response to any given situation. An emotion can even become a cellular memory toward a particular experience, triggering an emotional response when a similar situation arises. For example, suppose a person goes to the grocery store and becomes overwhelmed by the environment's energy. In that case, they may feel various emotions, such as fear, anxiety, and uneasiness. The power of those emotions becomes stored within the body, and they get filed away within the subconscious. The next time they go to the grocery store, they could begin to feel anxious, fearful, and uneasy in anticipation of returning to the store. They don't even have to go into the store. Their body has a trauma response, and the emotions flow without having to re-live the experience.

Suppose a person doesn't have the awareness that there is a loop potentially being created. In that case, they will feel anxious about going to the store. In severe situations, the person may never want to go to the store again. This can become a compounded loop and translate to going out to any public place, which, unfortunately, many people are stuck within. When our emotions dictate our lives, it can become detrimental to our well-being. Sometimes, we can become prisoners due to the emotional frequency that we are experiencing. If fear is the emotional frequency at which we are resonating, our mind, body, and spirit are also connected to that vibration. Our cells will replicate at that frequency, which may cause dis-ease.

Emotions can have a density as well. Lower vibrational emotions feel heavy and toxic to the body. The common saying, *you feel like you have the weight of the world on your shoulder*, comes from the heaviness of the worries we can carry with us that weigh us down. Sometimes, it can feel like immense pressure on your back, like an elephant sitting on your shoulders. The following illustrates how the more trapped emotions we have within our body, the heavier they feel.

HIGHER STATES OF CONSCIOUSNESS

Profound healing occurs when we achieve deep levels of relaxation. The reason for this is that when our body is in a relaxed state, the conscious mind can rest. When the conscious mind doesn't intervene, it is easier to connect to our higher self, communicate with our guides, and receive our most significant downloads. Have you ever been doing a nominal activity that doesn't require too much thinking, drifting off in thought, and suddenly, voila, you received the answer to something? That is called a download, where you receive information from your higher self or from one of your guides. Much like downloading a file to your computer, energetically, we can do the same thing with information. However, it is really hard to do that when we are bombarded with thoughts.

When our conscious mind is active, thousands of thoughts flow through our consciousness stream throughout the day. With all that activity, it's hard to receive downloads. There is too much interference. That is why people have the most potent activations and downloads while in meditation. The thing about mediation is that there are a lot of misconceptions out there that make it impossible for anyone to feel like they are doing it right. When I work with clients, I explain many ways to relax the mind. There is no right or wrong way to meditate. It's about quieting the mind. That can be achieved through exercise, yoga, singing, writing, listening to music, walking in nature, or being creative. It might be a process of trial and error before you find what works for you. You might also find different methods that work at various times, depending on the level of relaxation you are trying to reach.

Meditation is a personal experience, and there is no rule that it must be done sitting still and chanting. Personally, my favorite way to meditate and clear my mind is when I go running. I have received some of my most significant downloads while running. Sometimes, it is helpful to release expectations and hold the intention that you are open to receiving any guidance for your highest good while doing the activity of your choice. This relieves the pressure of going into the experience with a set of questions. That way, you won't feel blocked if you don't get the answers you seek. That simply is not always the case. Suppose you try to free your mind and open yourself up to receiving guidance not limited to a particular question. You may be surprised by how much information comes through in that case. You might even have breakthroughs you were not expecting, to things that were far more important.

At this point, you are likely asking: *how do I achieve more profound levels of relaxation?* First, I think it is essential to explain the stages of relaxation so you can identify how far you can go at any given moment. There are different stages of relaxation or levels to connect to your higher self and to your guides. The deeper in relaxation you are, the higher your frequency will be. As you move through the levels of consciousness, you will feel lighter, and your mind will become quiet. The stillness of the mind is what allows the messages to come through. There are four primary levels of hypnosis, which promote a higher state of consciousness.

Beta

This is the stage of relaxation when you begin to drift off. This happens to us when we start daydreaming. This can occur when you are in school while the teacher is talking, and you drift off, and your mind wanders. You can still hear their voice but are not retaining the lesson. Daydreaming is a form of connecting to your higher consciousness in an awake state. Children do this a lot because they are so multidimensional. They can alter their awareness and be in two places simultaneously with minimal relaxation. They might be asked to read a paragraph in a book, and once they finish, they don't remember anything they've read. That's because the monotony of reciting the words relaxed them just enough for their mind to wander. They were reading, but they weren't paying attention to the story.

The dark players introduced the Tel-lie-vision to hook people into the *programming* to receive subliminal messaging during the beta state. This is the case for any TV show or movie. That is why there are so many cartoons made by a well-known company that have countless subliminal messages and words hidden within the images that may not be noticeable to the naked eye. However, the subconscious can pick up on subtle cues in a relaxed state.

The beta state is a low-level state of relaxation where the brain waves are anywhere from 14 to 30 Hz. However, it shifts from the normal waking state to a progressively more relaxed state. It can promote a powerful connection to the higher self for short periods. It is a great way to start, and at first, when you try to relax, you may only be able to get to this point. That is perfectly ok because the more comfortable you become with beta, the easier it is to move on to alpha.

Alpha

The alpha state of relaxation is a little deeper than the beta state. At this level, you might experience time distortion or loss of time. An example is when you are driving a car and suddenly realize you have made it home but you don't remember the drive. Your mind wandered off enough so that you could disconnect from the experience of driving while still being able to drive the car. Your brain waves slow down to a rate of 8-13hz in the alpha state. The mind can slow down, and you begin to feel a sense of peace and calm. This state of consciousness allows much more information to be transmuted through your higher self and your guides.

Most people can reach alpha when doing yoga or any right-brain activity, such as crafting, painting, and listening to calming music. During most forms of meditation, a level of alpha is achievable. One of my favorite right-brain activities is automatic writing, where you intend to receive higher guidance, put your pen to paper, and write what comes to your mind. You don't read what you write. You trust in the information flowing through your consciousness, and you don't stop until you feel like you have reached a natural stopping point.

During the alpha state, people will still be aware of their surroundings. They will be able to respond to outside stimuli. Yet, they're tapped into another energetic space where their light body is activated. This energetic space is less physical and more multi-dimensional.

Theta

The theta state is a deeper level of relaxation where the brain waves are between 4-8hz. When a person goes deeper into meditation, they are generally within this state of consciousness. The body becomes much more relaxed, tension leaves the body, and a person enters a trance state. This is the level of relaxation that most hypnotherapists guide their clients so that they are very calm but not too relaxed that they fall asleep. Within this state of consciousness, a person can connect with their higher self and their guides much more clearly. During these periods, they may experience visions, full downloads, or spontaneous awakenings.

Delta

The delta state is the deepest level of relaxation, where the brain waves are between 0.5 to 4hz. If a person is in a deep delta level, they are likely asleep. This is when the body regenerates and heals itself. In the unconscious space, the body is idle mode, where cells regenerate, and the nervous system reboots. There is a space within delta that is called the lucid state, where you can connect to your higher self more profoundly. In the lucid state of consciousness, you are between awake and asleep and deeply relaxed. This is the level of relaxation that is referred to as Samadi, where the mind is clear, and everything around you is still. I believe this is where you can easily connect with the collective consciousness to access just about anything you want to know. In delta, there is no duality. It's just a space of neutrality, pure energy, and light.

WHAT IS YOUR BODY
TRYING TO TELL YOU?

Our body can tell us many things about our health because it continuously receives energetic signals. As our frequency fluctuates throughout the day based on our emotional response to experiences, we can either process the energy or hold on to it. For example, imagine a woman getting into an argument with her spouse. They argue about something that causes her to feel judged, angry, and defensive. In that moment, her body has shifted into a frequency that matches those emotions, which can be anywhere between 50 to 150hz. Let's say she must get to work, so they cannot resolve the argument, and she holds in those emotions because she can't process them at that moment. She goes to work feeling upset, potentially regretting things she said, or simply in a space of not caring. Either way, she didn't do anything to get the emotionally charged energy out of her body; therefore, it became trapped.

How long it remains trapped is up to her. She may decide to stop at the gym on her way home. She can release much pent-up energy from that morning's argument through intense breathing and exercise. This release can promote a more balanced state, so when she goes home, she will be less defensive when talking to her husband. Unfortunately, for many reasons, most people don't prioritize time for energetic release, so over time, there are a lot of trapped emotions in the body, which causes dis-ease in the long term.

Another issue I have found is the overwhelming number of people I have worked with over the years that are living to survive.

Their body cannot remain in balance, so it is constantly in a state of stress; therefore, it cannot take the time to heal. I will give you an example to explain the cause and effect regarding survival mode and healing. Think about a gazelle that is being chased by a cheetah. In that moment, the gazelle is in sympathetic mode and is running for his life. The body only focuses on pumping blood quickly so that he can breathe and circulate blood to his muscles to run fast. His high adrenaline and cortisol levels shut down digestion and most other regulatory organs. At that moment, the body is not worried about thriving. It is simply functioning to survive. Now, while this gazelle is running for his life, the body does not address any injuries he has endured from the cheetah's claws because it is not a priority. It is not until later that if the gazelle gets away and his body perceives he is safe, he will switch to a parasympathetic mode where the body can heal his wounds.

Take this example and relate it to a constantly stressed human under insurmountable pressure. Their body will remain in a sympathetic mode most of the time. That is when we can experience adrenal fatigue and heightened cortisol levels. If the body is perceiving continuous threats, the body won't take the time to heal. Our body is responding as if a cheetah is always chasing us. This puts unnecessary stress on the body, and it won't switch to healing mode simply because it doesn't feel safe. Unfortunately, I feel like too many people are experiencing this, and it prevents them from truly healing.

I will share what I have learned over the years while doing energy healings and clearings with my clients that may help you discern your health ailments based on where they are in the body and the type of dis-ease you have or may have had throughout your life. I will also share my favorite techniques and methods of healing that are simple and easy to incorporate into your life. I believe many of these techniques can shift the body out of survival mode and into a space of healing and balance. If only we were taught these methods as children, we wouldn't feel so lost as adults. The good news is it's not too late.

I recommend creating a healing journal to keep notes and critical factors as you embark on your healing journey. As you connect the dots and key puzzle pieces, taking notes and keeping track of milestones will be beneficial. Create a list of your physical pain and ailments and where in the body they are located. You will likely notice key triggers, patterns, and emotional connections to your overall health as you keep track. Taking charge of your health and wellness is empowering, which is why the dark players have worked so hard to push Western medicine that doesn't promote holistic and spiritual healing. It is up to us to go within and trust our intuition and our body's ability to tell us what we need to know about our health. Only then will the inverted truths about medicine and wellness break down, and through our recollection of our ability to heal ourselves as a collective, we will ignite a power within us that will break down the existence of illness. We are unstoppable when we achieve optimal mind, body, and soul connections.

The left side of the body

I have learned that knowing what side of the body you have pain or disease can be an essential clue. The left side of the body is connected to your other lifetimes. Because we can have many lives simultaneously, we are connected to those different versions of ourselves through our spiritual blueprint. Over time, the veil has thinned between timelines, so the separation between lives has decreased significantly. A thin veil has caused bleed-throughs of traumas, which can affect us at a cellular level. For example, if a person had lung cancer in another life and their soul has not healed from that experience, a cellular imprint can remain. This imprint can sit dormant within the person's spiritual DNA. When they are reborn in another life, it can become embedded in the physical DNA. Depending on the person's lifestyle or if they make similar choices as in the previous life, the imprint can become triggered. This can create a replay of lung cancer, heart conditions, or a chronic lung condition such as COPD, to give you a few examples.

Multidimensionality can become very complicated when you look at everything all at once. All aspects of our consciousness are connected through energetic patterns and cords. Much like blood vessels within the body, our lifetimes are connected by an intricate system of energetic pathways. The left side of the body can be an indication that we are receiving signals from other lifetimes that are not healed. Suppose a person has chronic pain in the left shoulder, hip, wrist, left breast, or anything located on the left side of the body. In that case, it can be a sign of interference from another life. Because we are in an ascension timeline, there is a heavy concentration on overall soul healing. There seems to be a common theme that people are doing much of their soul healing in this life. That is a lot to take on in one life, and it doesn't help that almost everything within the 3D box is designed to cause dis-ease and disbalance. 3D interference makes our healing journeys feel like an impossible uphill battle.

The right side of the body

The right side of the body is connected to our current life. If you have anxiety or fear that is directly linked to this life, the pain or ailment will present on the right side of the body. This means that there are trapped emotions within the body from this lifetime that need to be cleared. If there is right side body pain, it means that either you are holding on to trauma or resisting the surrendering process. Our body does what it can to give us the necessary signals. If we are paying attention, we can use them as clues to redirect our attention inward. We don't have to know exactly what emotion we are holding onto; although many of us can guess, there can be layers to it. Our primal instinct is to look outward when there is a problem in our life or a challenge. We perceive threats, and then we react to them. I have learned that it is much more impactful to shift our attention to our reactions and why we respond to experiences differently. Those are clues that can help us discern the lesson. The sooner we learn the lesson, the sooner we can move on to something else.

The right side of our body is an energy meter and an alert system for the present moment and our past. When we pay close attention to it, it can feel like our body has a specific language and communication system where pain is not always bad. Our body sends us signals to let us know we are on the right track and warn us of threats. If you notice that most of your pain and ailments are on the right side of your body, you know you have trapped emotional energy to work through this life.

The middle of the body

The middle of the body shares a delicate balance between the present and the parallel aspects of our consciousness. It's the halfway point between *the now* moment and the multidimensional version of us that can be in many places at once. If a person has ailments focused on the spine, the center thorax, sacrum, nose and throat, thyroid, lymphatics, and circulation. In that case, these can signify a combination of healings occurring in more than one life at a time.

Over the years, I have learned to pay attention to the location of my client's injuries, pain, and acute and chronic issues because they give important clues. Suppose someone suffers from an acute injury or condition. In that case, it is likely a new energy pattern or trauma trigger that is surfacing because it is now time for that person to embrace a new level of healing. A chronic issue is often a resistance or a block that prevents a person from putting in the time to heal. This will only amplify the dis-ease; until it's addressed, it will remain or intensify.

BODY TALK

The following is a short list of common health issues that humans have due to dis-ease within the 3D. There is a significant amount of 3D interference and influence and environmental toxins that contribute to these conditions; however, there is also an energetic explanation that I will share with you. One thing modern medicine is lacking is deciphering the root cause of illness. I believe that the root cause of any dis-ease is energy and emotions. Our energetic and spiritual hygiene is just as important as taking care of our bodies. When mindful of our energetic and physical aspects, we are more likely to be in harmony where illnesses cannot thrive. Our indigenous ancestors navigated illnesses very differently than we do today. They understood the physical body operates at its best when there is peace within the mind, body, and soul. Somewhere along the line, the soul was removed from the equation, and we were only taught about the connection between the body and mind.

I would even take it further to say that in modern days, the focus is on the body, and the mind has been removed. The mind has such a powerful effect on the body that it has the potential to influence our health. We are taught in school that nutrition and exercise are critical factors in our health. Yet, our food is bombarded with harmful chemicals, hormones, and toxins. The dark players have pushed fast food, soda, and sugar, as well as indoor and sedentary lifestyles where our mind is occupied by social media, watching movies, and playing video games. The normalization of pharmaceuticals has created an era of quick fixes where the side effects are written off as expected, and more medication is prescribed to mask the new symptoms. The real issues are not being addressed because the soul has been disregarded, and the mind is constantly distracted.

In my sessions with children, I have seen patterns of illness that have less to do with 3D interference and more to do with their high frequency. Much like toxic shock, there is a disconnect between the life force and the body's ability to receive the frequency coming through. This can cause a lot of the illnesses we see today. I have also seen a shift in adults who are awakening and activating to their peak frequency, which is causing acute and chronic health conditions like those of children. I think this is a unique and interesting perspective, that in combination with the 3D's toxic effect on humans, there is, in fact, a deeper explanation.

Inflammation

We have seen a massive shift in the collective awakening in the last ten years, and, as a result, a lot of the 3D interference is no longer working. Humanity is beginning to see through the illusion, triggering spontaneous activations, and the life force of our souls is starting to shine through. As we connect to our higher self, the pathway of energy increases and illuminates, and we become more powerful. If the body is not in an optimal space to receive an increase of light, the body can't react and resist. This can manifest in many ways, but the most common is inflammation. The entire body is suddenly on high alert as it tries to process the information coming through. When more light enters the body, it sends a rush of new energy and light codes. These light codes reprogram the cells to replicate in a higher frequency. Inflammation is an overall indication that there is a lack of harmony within the body.

If there is a sudden increase in energy, it can cause bronchitis, appendicitis, the flu, an ingrown toenail, arthritis, fibromyalgia, and infections. Nerve pain and joint pain are common signs that there is heavy inflammation within the body. It means there is too much light in the body, and a release needs to occur in order to reduce the pressure on the body. Sometimes, our body generates illness so the body can remove the energy. The flu is an excellent example of this. When our body heats up and removes toxins and trapped energy in the body through sweat, vomiting, phlegm, diarrhea, and urination, our body is healing and releasing. This is an example of how our body innately knows how to heal itself by purging the old energy to make way for new energy. Unbeknownst to the dark players, the COVID-19 pandemic was simultaneously an opportunity for a mass purging and awakening for thousands of people. Unfortunately, not all bodies were ready for that level of activation, so their souls transitioned in order to ascend.

There are situations when our bodies must get rid of specific physical matter in the body that is holding onto too much trauma. Appendectomies are an example of this. The appendix is connected to the sacral and root chakra, the energy centers most connected to fear and trauma. Suppose the appendix becomes filled with too much dense energy from stored trauma. In that case, it becomes inflamed and needs to be surgically removed. Although this can be quite a scary experience, it can be a powerful method to release energy trapped in the body. I have seen similar cases with my clients who have had tumors removed, hysterectomies, lung lobectomies, prostatectomies, and nephrectomies, to name a few.

Chronic inflammation can signify long-term disharmony within the mind, body, and soul, where deeper investigation is needed to discern the energetic cause. There may be more than one reason a person experiences inflammation, which may seem difficult. Still, I can assure you that underlying energetic patterns and factors can be identified. A loop or pattern triggered by a specific experience or life event is likely occurring. I recommend writing down everything relating to the inflammation, such as where it is located, when it started, what was happening during that period, what has changed or progressed since then, and other details you can gather. Add these details to your journal as tiny puzzle pieces. Eventually, you will begin to make sense of them when you connect the more significant pieces.

Inflammation within the body can give a lot of clues, and there are ways to assist energy movement throughout the body to promote balance and synergy between the soul's light and the physical body. Different grounding techniques combined with mild exercise and movement can assist with heavy surges of light entering the body. I am seeing a large percentage of my clients have sequences of mini-activations which are causing acute inflammation within the body, and people are being guided to surrender to the discomfort and try to utilize the information coming through in productive ways. As we activate, our right brain is stimulated, and we are encouraged to use that energy to create. There are no limitations, whether we make new music, art, books, or business plans, learn a new modality, meditate, do yoga and movements, or set an intention to co-create new energy for the collective.

Inflammation can be a sign that there are high levels of toxins and trapped energy within the body; however, it can also mean that high frequency light travels through us. The good news is that the protocols are the same, whether the reason is good or negative. Clean up your diet, release trapped emotions, surrender to the challenges in your life, create firm boundaries, develop good spiritual hygiene practices, reduce your dependency on Western medicine, and strengthen your connection to your divine self. Everything else will fall into place. I will share my favorite techniques with you later in this book when I get into specific healing methods.

Skin

Our skin is probably one of the most essential organs related to our frequency. The skin is the pathway between our physical body and our light body. As energy flows through the energy body into the physical body through the chakras, our skin acts as a barrier between the two. Our auric field is expansive, and the higher our frequency, the broader our light field can shine. Children have an auric field of up to 10-12 feet. Most adults have an auric field of 4-6 feet. A person with a low frequency of dis-ease within the body and a low sense of self can have an auric field only one foot in diameter around their body. Their energy is dense, scattered, and unpredictable. These people tend to have a lot of shadow beings and entities feeding off their energy because, to them, the low frequency is optimal to loosh from.

Some animals, such as dolphins and horses, can expand their energy frequency the length of a football field, which is why they make great therapy animals. They are oozing love and healing energy from them. One of my happiest moments in this life was when I swam with a family of dolphins. I had the opportunity to hug a dolphin while in the water, and I have never felt more at peace. There are no words to describe the emotions I felt. That dolphin let me hug him as long as I wanted. It's as if he merged his energy with mine and was happy to hold the space for whatever I needed. I even get emotional while writing about that day because I had never felt that type of energy before, not even with the pure love and connection I have with my children. I think about that experience from time to time, how that beautiful dolphin spirit allowed me to feel pure love through his light, and how precious that moment was for me. I often wonder if everyone on the planet could feel pure, unfiltered love like that at least once in their life and if it would wake them out of the 3D illusion.

I shared that experience because the skin is such a special organ that allows us to feel love with thousands of nerve endings. It can amplify the experiences we are having tenfold. That moment with the dolphin was an experience I felt through many senses. Still, the ability to touch and connect with that animal took it to a whole other level. Our skin has so many sensory processing abilities that it can positively amplify our experiences but can also be overwhelming. Many Starseeds have difficulty with touch and can be very sensitive to different textures and temperatures. That's why children labeled with autism have a high rate of sensory processing disorders because the stimuli from the outside world can be overwhelming. The feeling of the ground beneath their feet, the wind on their face, the textures of sand, slime, rough edges, different foods in their mouth, and various temperatures can be overstimulating. They feel much more profoundly than many 3D people anchored to this reality and used to the environment. High density beings are not connected to the 3D box and are sensitive to many things because their senses are heightened.

The skin can hold information, such as light codes from the Sun, spiritual blueprints, and data from the environment. Suppose the physical body isn't in a balanced state with optimal health. In that case, it can be difficult for the skin to hold this energy and integrate it with the physical body. If there is a disconnect between the light body and the physical body, it can cause the skin to react. When people get hives, acne, eczema, and psoriasis, it can be a sign of dis-balance between the physical and energetic aspects of the soul inhabiting the body. A conflict occurs, and the skin is the referee between the two. Resistance comes from the physical body, which cannot hold the frequency from which the outer body vibrates. The skin can also react due to toxins, poor diet, allergens, and environmental stressors; however, there is often a much bigger issue at hand.

There are things people can do to try and balance the body so that it can hold more light, such as limiting toxic and processed foods and sugars, avoiding sunblock, reducing or avoiding sunglass usage, taking breaks from electronics, reducing EMFs in the home, releasing judgement of others, and shifting your mindset. Remove yourself from *fight-or-flight* mode by releasing expectations, surrendering, going out in nature more often, sitting in the sun, taking salt baths, and mindful breathing can release trapped emotions weighing you down. Combining all these things can help the body release, balance, and prepare to shift into a higher density. There is no doubt that humanity is moving to a higher frequency. As a result, the body is shifting into a higher density where it can hold more light. The skin is the vessel of transmission between the outer and inner worlds, which is a good indicator of resistance or something you need to pay attention to.

Hair

During my sessions over the years, I have learned some fascinating things about hair. One of the first sessions I had where hair was brought up was with a middle-aged woman obsessed with hair. She refused to cut her hair as a child, and when her parents made her trim her hair, she would cry, and her parents didn't understand why it was such a big deal. During hair trims, she would say that it hurt, but her parents knew that cutting hair didn't cause pain because hair doesn't have nerve endings. They would get upset with her and would tell her to stop making up *"such nonsense,"* as they would put it. Eventually, she gave up fighting, and it wasn't until she was an adult that she grew her hair long and would only trim a tiny amount once a year in January to start the new year fresh. She became obsessed with braids and always had her hair in one long braid.

In the session, she wanted to know why she felt so connected to her hair and why she would cry as a child when her parents would cut it. I was shown a life where she was a native American female with hair down to her bottom. Her hair was in three sections, with three braids down her back. I received many flashes of her life and was shown how significant the hair was to Native Americans. It was considered a continuation of the physical body, which stores energy and information. It's very similar to teeth, where they regarded their hair as keepers of their wisdom and experience. The hair was an extension of themselves, so they only cut hair if there was a death or trauma. Cutting the hair signified significant loss, mourning, and the end of a chapter. This was a process of grief, and the hair was kept in a cedar box and treasured, much like those that hold teeth.

When my client was a child, she would cry during haircuts. I believe she was experiencing a cellular memory of that life where she knew subconsciously that cutting her hair was a painful process. A piece of her was being cut from her body, and it could have actually caused her the sensation of pain through grief. Throughout the years, I have had countless sessions with clients connected to lives as Native Americans and indigenous tribes. They all value hair as a significant part of their spiritual beliefs. I have had clients who were enslaved, and as a sign of being dominated and controlled, their hair was cut short. It was a humiliating and abusive ritual to enslave Indigenous people.

In another session, I was told that the American military began cutting soldier's hair in an attempt to strip them of their identity. The longer the hair, it is believed, the greater your wisdom and experience. It makes sense that if a person is being initiated into the military, the leaders would want to strip them of their independence. I believe that boot camp is like resetting your smartphone to factory settings. During this process, you remove the part of the phone that is *you*, the pictures, the messages, the apps, and the personalization. Then, you restore the original factory settings that the phone came with. When you go into some military boot camps, it seems as though they are trying to strip the identity of the person. Through a process of cutting off their hair, having everyone dress precisely the same, constant yelling and demeaning, sleep deprivation, harsh training, and little to no communication with the outside world, their soul ultimately fragments. When this occurs, the group of recruits becomes one unified group with a hive mentality.

I deeply value and respect our military. I have family on both sides who have served, dear friends who are veterans, and close friends who are newly enlisted. My intention with the previous paragraph was not to put down the military; however, I wanted to explain how cutting off a person's hair, as well as other military training tactics, can strip a person of their energetic and physical identity. I don't see these tactics being used in the future quantum military. I see a massive shift in how our military is trained, respected, supported, and valued.

Our hair is such a significant part of our physical body, and there are many ways our hair can assist in our healing. Each strand of our hair has the capability of receiving light codes from the Sun. It's as if there are little antennas that channel energy toward the body, which can be processed through the brain. When we cut our hair, our body uses vitamin D, phosphorus, and calcium to regrow, which it pulls from other areas. When our hair is longer and not actively growing, the body can use those vitamins and minerals for energy and endurance.

I believe that people have utilized hair as an opportunity to express their unique nature, their culture, and their state of being. Native Americans braid their hair with three strands to signify the connection of the mind, body, and spirit. Some cultures in Africa place their hair in a spiral above their head with the intention that the hair becomes an extension of themselves. Some cultures believe that hair acts as an antenna. If placed in a certain way, it can receive energy from the universe that will travel down their hair and into the spine. Straight hair can signify balance, strength, wisdom, and empowerment. Wavy hair can signify transformation, change, or an easy-going state of being. Curly hair can signify deep wisdom being held tightly within the curls, resilience, and a sense of power. Coarse hair can represent triumph, perseverance, and indigenous roots. Even the color of our hair can reveal necessary information—red hair stores ancient knowledge of our ancestors and rare wisdom. Black hair represents wisdom, strength, and firm boundaries. Brown hair represents growth, resilience, and determination. Blond hair represents purity and wonder. White hair represents transformation and freedom.

There are a lot of different belief systems throughout the world, but one consistency is that hair is important. In modern days, it is common to see men with short hair. Many women have short hair as well. It is common to see people dyeing their hair in different colors and putting a variety of products in their hair to style it in a specific way. There are many barber shops and salons in cities where hair is trimmed and swept away into the trash without considering its energetic impact. I believe the dark players know the significance of hair, which is why there is a heavy influence on hairstyles that celebrities, models, and influencers push into the collective. Celebrities introduce different fads; the next thing we see are thousands of influential fans dyeing their hair blue or wearing it in a certain way. This creates a narrative that hair is simply an accessory and nothing more. Introducing harsh dyes and chemicals through the hair and into the scalp can cause various health issues, such as headaches, rashes, and neurotoxicity.

Looking back a few generations, the masses follow whatever hairstyles, hair colors, clothing, make-up, and cars the elite have. We see suggestive programming in magazines, TV, movies, and on social media. This could also be the reason that, in recent generations, the notion of no body hair or facial hair has become normalized. Perhaps the dark players believe it is best to reduce the amount of body hair we have so we are less likely to connect to *any* energetic benefits of hair, regardless of where it grows.

My personal opinion is that hair holds energy and information. Hair is alive, just like anything else in our body. I believe that having longer hair increases the ability to receive light codes, downloads, and knowledge. I have experienced it myself, so I trim my hair once a year and prefer to keep it long. However, that does not mean that a person with short hair or no hair loses the ability to receive light codes, downloads, and knowledge. There is always more than one pathway to enlightenment. As we have evolved as a species, we have adapted. With generations of people wearing their hair shorter, I think we have found other ways to receive messages and data from the universe. Through breath work, intention, grounding, and raising our frequency, we have other ways to connect. So, if you have short hair, don't feel like you are at a disadvantage. Perhaps you have found other, more profound ways to connect.

Teeth

I have learned much about our teeth and how they relate to our spiritual blueprint. Much like elephant tusks, teeth hold information. They are filled with memories, light codes, and energy. Our teeth are the record keepers of life. Much like the Akashic records, teeth are filled with essential data that can't be destroyed. Throughout our lives, energy travels through our teeth. During times of trauma, dense energy can become trapped within the tooth cavities, causing infections and tooth pain. Drinking water with fluoride and consuming large amounts of sugar can break down the teeth's enamel and integrity. The damage from prolonged tooth decay can cause a weakness in the blueprints, which hold valuable information. There are so many distorted truths about oral health and the maintenance of our teeth. Modern dentists push fluoride usage and harsh procedures, such as root canals, extractions, wisdom teeth removal, and radiation exposure with annual X-rays.

I am not a dentist, nor am I giving medical advice. However, throughout countless sessions and conversations with holistic dentists,

I have learned a lot about the misconceptions of oral hygiene and proper oral care. I have been told that the pathway to the internal body begins with the skin and the mouth. Suppose the mouth is not treated as a protective and sacred entrance to the body, our temple. In that case, we are inviting negativity and dis-ease. Starting with food, our ancestors ate from the land, so their diet had minimally processed ingredients. There were no harsh sugars or foreign ingredients that would attack the teeth. In modern days, sugar and processed foods are a significant part of the food industry; therefore, our teeth are exposed to un-natural syrups, dyes, acids, gummies, gels, hard candy, toxins, and chemicals.

In the United States, fluoride was introduced to the public water supply around 1945. I was told that the dark players added it to water after they discovered it was a way to lower IQ, block the pineal gland, and sedate large amounts of people. The dark players are always looking for ways to suppress people so they can more easily be controlled. The pineal gland is a significant part of our human anatomy and physiology that connects the spirit to the body. Our pineal gland works closely with the cerebral spinal fluid, which, I explained in my previous book, is the only physical part of the human design that holds our consciousness. The delicate pathway of information that flows through the pineal gland, connected to the crown and third eye chakras, flows into the spine via the cerebral spinal fluid, down the sacred vertebra of the body, connecting to all the main chakras. This is the divine pathway to our soul and higher levels of consciousness.

I believe that the dark players understood if the pineal gland is calcified from fluoride, the intuitive and multidimensional aspect of the human race would become blocked. Once a species cannot think for itself, it becomes dependent on its leaders, becoming docile and subservient. To make things worse, fluoride was added to toothpaste in the 1970s, which only amplified the exposure. This initiated a campaign to spread misinformation on the false benefits of fluoride to the collective. Dentists were indoctrinated to push the fluoride agenda into their practices.

The list of harmful effects from fluoride exposure is too numerous to list, but I will share some of them here:

- Bone weakness

- Dental fluorosis (white or brown spots on teeth)

- Receding and sensitive gums

- Calcification of the pineal gland

- Skeletal fluorosis (metabolic bone and joint disease)

- Lowers IQ

- Impairs the immune system

- Sedates and causes fatigue

- Mental disturbances

- Attacks thyroid

- DNA damage

- Alzheimer's connection (fluoride causes the body to absorb extra aluminum, which goes to the brain. Alzheimer's patients have high levels of aluminum)

If our body is a temple and our teeth are the record keepers, it is safe to say that our oral health is essential. Because massive amounts of energy flow through our mouths every day and the most critical information is stored within each of our teeth, it is expected that trauma can also become trapped there. Suppose we have a tremendous amount of stress, anxiety, fear, and trauma throughout our lives, which many people do. In that case, our teeth can become overwhelmed. I believe this is where toothaches, grinding, and conditions such as TMJ (temporomandibular joint dysfunction) come from. Our teeth tell us we have too much of something trapped inside, and it needs to come out. Now, if we were to eliminate the outside toxins as much as possible, such as fluoride, sugars, and chemicals, our teeth would be much stronger. Even so, many of us would still endure hardship and traumas that would put a significant amount of strain on our teeth. So many layers must be dissected and broken down to truly innerstand the connections.

Wisdom teeth are another layer of deceit and inverted truths narrated by the dark players. The teeth in our mouths mostly hold information from our current lives. In contrast, our wisdom teeth hold data from many lifetimes. They serve as lifelines that connect us to our other lives. Our wisdom teeth hold generations of wisdom within each of us. Our teeth are the only body parts not destroyed during cremation or the natural decaying process. Much like elephant tusks, crystals, and rocks, our teeth will always carry codes of valuable information for our ancestors to unlock when the time is right.

I believe our ancient human ancestors had a much larger frame and could be 10 to 12 feet tall. Because of this, we had much more room in our mouths to hold the wisdom teeth, which were an essential part of our genetic and spiritual blueprint. Over time, and due to genetic modification, our frames got smaller. A theory for this is that it is much easier for the dark players to control humanity when their bodies are smaller, less strong, less intelligent, and more dependent as a species. Because our heads get smaller, there is less room for our teeth, so the wisdom teeth have become too big to fit in our jaw structure. It is my opinion that this was done by design so they would have an excuse to take our wisdom teeth from us. This is yet another agenda to steal our innate wisdom. The crazy thing is that not everyone needs to have their wisdom teeth removed. Some people naturally have a more prominent jaw to accommodate the extra molars; however, many are convinced that removing their wisdom teeth is part of routine oral care.

The story of the tooth fairy is a clue as to the various ways our teeth were honored by our ancestors. In Norse mythology, children's teeth were given symbolically to Odin in exchange for protection. Vikings would also wear teeth around their neck to bring good luck when they went into battles. In European cultures, they will burn their lost teeth to protect the child in their afterlife and to protect them from witches. I find this interesting because teeth can't actually be destroyed. However, their belief is what gives this process power. Witches are believed to use teeth to cast spells on a person. Spanish cultures use the symbol of a rat because a rat's teeth never stop growing. Many believe teeth bring good luck and will offer them to mice, birds, and other Gods. So, why all the fuss about teeth if they aren't special?

I can recommend a few things to help you maintain a healthy and balanced sacred space for your mouth and teeth. The first and most important thing is to discontinue fluoride toothpaste and mouthwash. There are plenty of non-fluoride toothpaste options. You can also make your toothpaste by combining ingredients such as coconut oil, bentonite clay, activated charcoal, clove oil, baking soda, and peppermint essential oil. Secondly, avoid harsh mouthwashes full of toxic and harsh ingredients that can aggravate the gums and tooth enamel. Instead, coconut pulling is a very effective way to clear bacteria from the mouth. Place a teaspoon of coconut oil in your mouth and swoosh it like mouthwash. The longer you do it, the more beneficial it can be. I recommend five minutes as the least amount of time and up to 20 minutes for the maximum benefits. Once you are done, spit all the contents into the trash bin or outside. Do not put it into the sink or toilet because, over time, the oils can clog the pipes.

Coconut pulling can assist in the pulling of toxins and bacteria as well as trapped energy within the teeth and mouth. Daily coconut pulling can bring your oral care to the next level. I have clients who have experienced a dramatic decrease in nerve pain and gum sensitivity since they started coconut pulling. I even had a parent whose son had cavities at every dental visit, completely shifted his oral health once he started coconut pulling, and he never got another cavity. There are so many natural ways we can care for our teeth that we are not taught. I think it's important to remember the significance and the information that is stored within our teeth. Then, we will realize how they are connected to our spiritual DNA as mini record keepers of stored consciousness. I can see us shifting how we value and care for our teeth in the future. Whether we keep our teeth for ceremonies, burn them, or learn how to access the information stored within them like crystal balls, I believe it will look completely different than it does today.

Autoimmune Disorders

Autoimmune disorders are another common energetic dissonance that occurs within the body. Whether a person has type 1 diabetes, lupus, celiac disease, Hashimoto's thyroiditis, inflammatory bowel disease, or multiple sclerosis, there is an energetic battle going on within the body. I have had countless sessions with clients who have been diagnosed with an autoimmune disorder, and I have received the same message repeatedly. I have been told that when there is a disconnect between the physical body and the light body, or when the frequency the soul is carrying is too high, the body goes into a severe form of *fight-or-flight* where it is not even sure what to attack because the perceived threat is unknown. In the medical field, we call this idiopathic because the cause is a mystery. Suppose a physician can't identify the origin of an illness. In that case, they will define it as a *disease of itself* or uncertain origin. There can be a list of symptoms but no clear indication of why the dis-ease is occurring.

It has been explained to me that the energetic integration process has been progressive and, in many circumstances, experimental. I have learned the most from my clients with an Arcturian connection in their soul lineage. I have had sessions where I have communicated with an Arcturian being, and they have shown me how human genetics have been studied for thousands of years and continue to be studied to the present day. They shared that many Starseeds with a density of consciousness far exceeding the human energetic capacity have agreed to volunteer to incarnate within human bodies to assist in a slow transition and activation of the collective DNA over time. With an experiment of this magnitude, there will be successes and failures. However, there is no such thing as failure because there is a certain level of trial and error required to reverse engineer thousands of years of negative genetic altering and manipulation. What better way to activate the human DNA than to have ascended souls with massive amounts of light incarnate in human bodies to bring in new generations of hybrids?

There is an extensive range of galactic beings incarnating as humans from the Pleiades, Lyra, Sirius, Orion, Andromeda, the Angelic realm, Alpha Centauri, Inner Earth, Jupiter, Venus, and other universes, which is having a profound impact on the acceleration of awakened souls within 3D. Our DNA is shifting and activating, causing the density of the human form to shift from carbon to crystalline, and as a result, the newer bodies can hold a higher density of consciousness. Human epigenetics is shifting rapidly to make room for more elevated states of consciousness that can anchor into the 5th dimension and beyond.

The process is gradual; as I mentioned, there can be setbacks. Not all bodies can thrive with a soul that carries a high frequency. Sometimes, a battle can occur where the body rejects the light coming through, an autoimmune condition. It appears the body is attacking healthy cells because, in a way, it is. When high light surges come through, and the body cannot interpret the data, it can short circuit. This translates as inflammatory bowel disease, for example, where the digestive tract becomes severely inflamed and can lead to infection and long-term management. The soul and the body must figure out how to work together, or failure to thrive will be the result. I have seen this with sudden miscarriages, infant death, and life-threatening auto-immune disorders where the person almost dies.

There are a few ways I have seen this play out. One option is for the soul to exit the body, come back through, and try again. This happens a lot with miscarriages. The soul will leave the body because the fetus cannot hold the frequency. In many cases, the mother is the one who needs to prepare her body to carry a higher frequency before the soul can come back. Another option is a reverse walk-in where the soul invites an angelic or more Earth-bound spirit to merge with their consciousness and stay within the body as it grows. The body will be able to go through vital developmental stages. When it is ready, the consciousness and energy of the original soul will begin the integration process until the time is suitable for the two souls to swap places. I spoke more about reverse walk-ins in my previous book, *Starseeds and the Great Awakening.*

Another option is a slow integration, which is common among adults and some children. The soul will retract a good percentage of their light so that the body only receives a small amount at a time to give it time to adjust in shifts. Over time, more and more of their light will integrate with the body. This has a higher rate of success, but the person with the autoimmune disorder must be ready to do the spiritual work alongside the physical wellness routine. It's not just about eating high vibe foods and exercising. The person must be willing to transition their lifestyle, account for emotional triggers, evaluate their relationship with themselves, see their limiting beliefs, and initiate surrendering so the body can heal and transition slowly.

I also see a lot of autoimmune disorders in my clients that have severely fragmented souls. Many souls have chosen this life to achieve deep levels of healing so they can facilitate a process of soul retrieval. If the soul is lost, and there are a lot of trauma patterns with low life force energy, it can trigger an autoimmune reaction as the healing process is facilitated. Just as I mentioned in the previous section, it doesn't necessarily matter why the autoimmune response was triggered; the important thing is to focus on how to move forward with more knowledge and innerstanding of how the body is processing new light codes coming through. Once you combine the spiritual element with the physical healing process, one can expect to see improvement little by little.

Obesity

According to my sessions, I have learned that the dark players initiated an agenda in the late 1990s that completely shifted the trajectory of human health. With the increase of fast food, processed food, sugar, toxins, and a more sedentary lifestyle among the masses, more and more people have become overweight. The higher the body mass index (BMI), the more fat is stored in the body, which causes an increase in weight. Being overweight puts more pressure on the spine, joints, bones, and muscles to support the extra weight. The organs and the body systems must work harder to maintain balance and strong immunity. This can cause physical symptoms, such as cardiovascular disease, type 2 diabetes, musculoskeletal disorders, chronic fatigue, and respiratory issues. This can take a toll on mental wellness, causing cloudy thoughts, lack of motivation, lack of confidence, depression, shame, guilt, envy, gluttony, bargaining, and many other emotions.

A combination of the physical, mental, and emotional side-effects of weight gain can lower a person's vibration significantly. When a person is overweight and feeling down, they are less likely to exercise or be active. They may even go into a shame spiral where they binge eat and feel regret and shame, and then start to exercise. Still, when they don't get the expected results, they binge again, thus creating a negative loop. Many people don't realize that the matrix is designed to hold people hostage within it, causing them not to realize that *they ARE the matrix.* The matrix is made up of our energy; therefore, we have the power to shift it. Because the dark players don't want that to click in our heads, they do what they can to dumb us down as much as possible. If our body works hard to stay alive, we are not thriving.

The dark players want us to be stuck within a low frequency that is optimal for them. To keep the collective resonating at its optimal vibration, they need to make us sick, dependent, vulnerable to suggestive programming, and divided. Obesity is one way they can create a society of dependent, unhealthy people who can't think for themselves. When large groups of people are in a vibration of shame, they are easy to program because they are vulnerable and weak. The dark players intensify this by inserting overweight and obese actors on TV and in movies. It has become socially acceptable to be overweight, and some singers and influencers push the agenda by parading their version of beauty around. This influences young minds to think they can eat unhealthily and become overweight and that it is entirely safe and normal. The term *fatphobic* has been circulating to shame people who discriminate against people with obesity.

I want to be clear that I am not saying a person needs to be thin to be beautiful. I am also not saying that all overweight people are manipulated. What I am saying is that there is a clear agenda set forth to sabotage the collective in redefining what is beautiful and socially accepted. This generation of children is bombarded with fast food, processed food, sodas, and sugary treats and are not properly being taught the negative health effects. Physical education has become an elective in many schools, and children are not getting enough exercise and outdoor activities. With technological advancements, children are coming home from school and getting on their screens, VR, and video games, and they are spending less time active and outside. In my generation, we spent all our time outside. We would ride our bikes for miles and get lost without cell phones, and we figured it out. We were much more in-tune with nature, and we enjoyed outdoor adventures.

The children of today are so misguided and disconnected because of countless agendas set forth by the dark players. Children are more sedentary, eating poor diets, and getting heavier and heavier. Children are developing illnesses younger than ever before. This has a lot to do with parasites, malnutrition, toxic EMF exposure, food and environmental poisons, heavy metals, vaccines, and so much more. Each generation becomes less healthy than the last, and obesity is a significant factor. Unfortunately, it starts with our children, who are led down a slippery slope of bad health habits. It is up to us to educate ourselves on genetically modified and bioengineered food, toxins, and parasites, and slowly take back our power. We can do this by growing our own mini-gardens, joining communities with shared gardens, and supporting local farmers' markets and small businesses. I believe there are options for every budget, even those in financial hardship who are eating to survive.

Food is another weapon of spiritual warfare that can be used in both directions. There are areas of the world that are deprived of food and are dying due to lack of nourishment. At the same time, other regions of the world are dying from obesity and overindulgence. Both scenarios achieve the same goal: a society dependent and vulnerable to a higher power that dictates its health and wellness through deprivation and manipulation. I am not just talking about first-world versus third-world countries. Division among provinces, states, cities, and even neighborhoods can exist. For example, I live in West Palm Beach, Florida. I can drive west from the beach and pass through three very different ranges of wealth, from the most elite to extreme poverty. There are 30-million-dollar homes on the beach, country clubs, fancy restaurants, and boutiques, and within just a few miles, neighborhoods are filled with homelessness, abandoned buildings, low-cost housing, and streets lined with liquor stores. As you travel west, you reach the middle-class neighborhoods with a completely different vibe than the wealthy and the poverty zones. You can always tell the level of economic status of a community by how clean and well-kept the roads and landscaping are, as well as the types of grocery stores, restaurants, and retail stores that are available. I rarely see fast food chains in wealthy areas, whereas many are in middle-class and lower-class regions.

A sad fact about the third dimension is that the more money a person has, the better-quality food they can access. With the recent political climate and attempts by the dark players to cut humanity off at their knees, the food industry has become volatile. No one knows what they can eat or what ingredients are in their food. People have lost trust in the mass food supply and the manufacturers, and rightfully so. Many families struggle to feed their families, so they are forced to buy whatever they can, depending on their budget. In this spiritual war, there are layers of deceit and control parameters. Food is most certainly used as a pawn in the game of 3D, and obesity is one element of the game that suits their rules. Many things in our reality may be out of our control; however, we can control our mindset and intentions. Despite 3D interference and 3D influence, we control our frequency, and there are ways to ensure their attacks don't work on us. I will share valuable tools to exercise our sovereignty later in this book.

Digestion

Digestive issues are common throughout the collective for many reasons. Energetically, the lower three chakras are connected to the digestive tract. The solar plexus, sacral, and root chakras are the energetic pathways to the digestive system, among other organs. The emotions associated with these chakras are fear, worry, guilt, shame, and rage. These emotional centers are affected by their sense of security, support, and stability. If a person doesn't have a solid foundation, they are in survival mode, and their body shifts into sympathetic mode. When that occurs, the body shunts blood to survival organs, and the digestive tract is not part of that vital system. Because of this, digestion comes to a halt or significantly slows down. Digestion is not a priority in a life-or-death response.

The problem is, in today's world, people are in survival mode most of the time, so their digestive tract does not function optimally. Stress responses can increase cortisol, which suppresses the digestive system. This has caused a lot of acute and prolonged digestive disorders over generations of time. Another reason for digestive malfunction is that our bodies don't know how to process and break down all the fake foods in our diet. Organic fruits, vegetables, meat, beans, and grains have a unique genetic code. When we eat a specific item, our body recognizes its genetic make-up and breaks it down. The body absorbs the nutrients and discards the waste. For example, when we eat an apple, our body immediately recognizes its genome and knows how to process it and absorb the vitamins and nutrients. When we eat processed food with many fake ingredients, the body receives it and doesn't know how to process it because it is trying to recognize what it is. There is no identifiable DNA or structure so the body will reject it. When the body rejects a particular food, the symptoms are stomachache, bloating, nausea, diarrhea, constipation, and vomiting.

The problem with modern food is that it is packed with synthetic ingredients, toxins, dyes, and poisons. With mass production and heavy preservatives, the quality of the food has been altered. Even whole foods like fruits and vegetables are sprayed with heavy pesticides and chemicals, which can be toxic to people and even strip the health benefits altogether. This causes the body to be in defense mode, leading to heartburn, stomach ulcers, and chronic digestive issues. This is why a significant percentage of the population suffers from some degree of digestive illness.

There is, however, an energetic explanation as well. Because many Starseeds are empaths, they are susceptible to the emotional shifts in others. Many people are tuned in to the frequency of others, and it can energetically and physically affect their health. Everyone's vibration oscillates throughout the day based on the environment and our emotional state. Because many people in our communities are going through hardship, many scattered emotions are circulating. If someone is in crowded public spaces frequently, their energy field can be affected.

For example, if a person works at the register at the grocery store, they are going to interact with a lot of people throughout the day. That means they are going to be exposed to many people's energy fields and those people's energetic entourage. There is a good chance that the person working will experience an array of emotions from people as they interact with them at check out. If that person is an empath and is sensitive to others' energy fields, there is a good chance they will be influenced by other people's negativity throughout the day. This can affect the lower chakras, causing stomach upset, inflammation and digestive upset.

Whether the root cause of digestive disorders is energetic, environmental, or a combination of the two, it is clear that our body is trying to tell us something. Sometimes, we need a good detox, parasite cleanse, and intermittent fasting to reboot the system. Changing our diet has a lot to do with optimal digestive health, so we should eat as many whole foods as possible. We have to go back to intuitive eating instead of *fad* dieting. I have never been a fan of diets because it is impossible to stick to something long-term. We constantly shift energetically throughout our lives; therefore, our bodies will crave and require different things depending on our needs. We must learn to pay attention to our cravings, what we are intuitively being guided to eat, how often and how much we eat. When we let our bodies guide us, we might eat less one day and crave only fruit, whereas the next day, we may feel the need to eat meat and carbs, and the next day, small portions of nuts and vegetables. It may not be as abrupt as I described; therefore, we must learn to listen to our bodies. We may even go through periods where we eat less or more than usual. We may even develop a distaste for things we have always liked or a sudden interest in something we used to hate.

Things can change, and we can develop sudden allergies to things we eat our entire lives, such as dairy. Sometimes, our bodies give us clues to let us know something is not suitable for us anymore. That stomachache we get after eating ice cream can indicate that limiting or eliminating dairy is necessary. The critical thing to remember is that things run in cycles, so just because you must lay off the dairy now doesn't mean it will always be that way. There may be some types of dairy that you can have and others that cause severe stomach agitation, likely related to the processing of the dairy. Intuitive eating is about paying attention to all clues to make better decisions.

The issue is that our society is designed with quick fixes, so instead of stopping dairy, we are given pills to help with the digestion of lactose or pills for bloating, gas, and heartburn. Those medications don't address the root cause of the issue. They only help mask the side effects of a genuine concern our body is trying to relay to us. The long-term effects of eating foods our body can't process are chronic digestive disorders such as GERD, Irritable Bowel Syndrome, Chronic Idiopathic Constipation (CIC), and Chron's disease.

We are also trained from an early age to hold in our feelings, to be good girls and boys, and not to cry or show weakness. Trapped emotions in our body can have a lasting impact on our ability to digest food because our body doesn't know how *to let go*. We are often so tense from stress and holding in our worries that our digestive system is in limbo, which can be the reason for constipation. Our emotional well-being can affect our digestive system. My best advice is to eat intuitively, eliminate fake food, take digestive enzymes, prebiotics, probiotics, do periodic parasite cleanses, detox from heavy metals, drink clean water free of fluoride, and practice letting go. Make a conscious effort to release anything you are holding on to that is no longer serving you. I will give more tips on this later in the book.

Ascension Symptoms

Many people are experiencing ascension symptoms, which are gradual shifts in their physical bodies as they adjust to new frequencies. With new light codes coming from the Sun, the collective consciousness shifting into higher densities, and the activation of dormant DNA, our bodies are transitioning to more crystalline than carbon. Essentially, we are becoming more *light* and less connected to the density of 3D. The *light bright* of the collective is illuminating, and the 3D box is breaking down a little at a time. As we shift into higher densities of consciousness, our bodies are shedding toxins, and our bodies are holding more light. This transition is causing a lot of symptoms that can range from mild to severe.

I will list the most common ascension symptoms that my clients are experiencing. This is not a complete list, but it will give you an idea of how our bodies process, transmute and prepare for a transition into a higher dimension. The important thing to know is that if you are experiencing any of the symptoms, it can be due to the ascension. Your body might be going through a series of shifts, each preparing your body for a new level of transition. Sometimes illnesses are perceived as setbacks when in reality, they can be validation that you are transmuting and transcending traumas. Consider your ailments as adjustments to new energy so your body can perceive higher dimensions. Your senses are adjusting to new tastes, sounds, sites, stimuli, and deeper levels of communication.

I am not a physician, nor do I suggest ignoring any of the symptoms below as non-threatening. I am simply sharing a list of common symptoms and emotions I have noticed with my clients, friends, my children, and myself. These are very likely adjustments and a vital process of ascension.

Common Ascension Symptoms

- Headache

- Dizziness

- Ringing in the ears

- Nose bleeds

- Forgetfulness/loss of memory

- Heart palpitations

- Weight gain

- Inflammation

- Joint pain

- Fatigue

- Vivid dreams

- Stomachache

- Colds or Flus

- Coughs

- Digestive issues

- Sensitivity to food/light/sound/touch

- Insomnia

- Abrupt changes in mood and/or interests

- Longing to do something more or feeling like you aren't doing enough

- Hair loss

- Sensitive skin (hives, psoriasis, alopecia)

CREATING BOUNDARIES

Creating boundaries is one of the most incredible things we can do for ourselves. I think if we were taught as children how important boundaries are and why they are necessary, we would have a lot less issues as adults. In my previous books, I have spoken a lot about energy, how people can directly affect each other's energy field, and how important it is to shield and protect ourselves. I don't want to repeat myself in this book, so I will do my best to offer more details and ways we can further protect ourselves.

Because every life form oscillates at a unique frequency, there are ranges and resonances of compatibility. When two or more people come together, their energetic bodies meet first.

This can be a pleasurable convergence of frequencies or disconcerting, depending on where everyone is resonating. I believe this is why a lot of people are struggling right now. As more and more people awaken, they become aware of their energy, environment, and triggers. Our perception is shifting, and as a result, it is becoming more apparent which relationships serve our highest good and those that don't. As the illusion breaks down, it becomes clear who the antagonists, bullies, narcissists, abusers, and energetic vampires are in our lives. As we begin to stand in our power and re-establish our sovereignty, we begin to recognize all our unhealthy habits and the people in our lives that have enabled us to be a weaker version of ourselves.

More and more people are losing friends, and their friendship circles are becoming smaller. I have countless clients who have lost all their friends during their awakening. What is important to realize right now is that there are three categories people are falling into during this ascension period. The ones that are ready to proceed, the ones that are on the fence, and the ones that refuse. Believe it or not, many 3D-bound souls do not wish to ascend to a higher density of consciousness. They are perfectly content with where they are, and there is nothing their lover, friend, parent, sibling, or child can say to them that is going to change their mind. For those of us in the *"let's do this"* category, we have to try our best to innerstand the free will of the seemingly lost souls and allow them to follow their own calling. Those are the people that are going to continue to make 3D choices. They will want to drink, party, and do drugs as often as they wish. They will make irresponsible decisions with no regard for others. If you have someone in your life like that, it is my recommendation that you create boundaries and distance yourself from them so that you can proceed on your path with no connections pulling you back.

I always say, "It's not bye forever; it's just bye for right now." I believe this is true for many families and friendships that have been torn apart. It is heartbreaking, but one of our biggest lessons in all of this is to save ourselves. That might sound selfish, but many of us are here to do ancestral healing for thousands of other souls. Many of us play a significant role in a movement that could affect millions and future generations. Because we don't know all the variables and reasons why a soul chooses to remain in 3D, it is best to send them love and then move in a different direction so that your mission doesn't become compromised.

I know it is not as simple as kicking people out of our lives because sometimes that's impossible. Perhaps you live with someone who is a narcissist, and you have nowhere else to go. Possibly, there are children stuck in the middle. Perhaps it's a parent, and you can't abandon them because you are all they have. There are so many reasons why walking away isn't an option. I innerstand that it's not that simple for everyone. In this case, I would practice energetic boundaries when you are around the person. I would not engage in controversial conversations, and I would not micromanage their life. If they are doing things you disagree with, instead of expressing it, put up energetic walls and focus on yourself. Agree to disagree; that way, a neutral territory will be established.

Because so many people walk around more in-tune with their energy and intuition, they notice how the outside world affects them. It is more evident to people now than ever how they can be shifted off balance when they are around someone at a lower frequency. All emotions and hormones have a frequency. Living in a house with someone who is anxious and has high cortisol levels can affect your body's cortisol levels. Suppose that person is resonating at the frequency of anxiousness. In that case, their body gives off energetic cortisol data within that frequency band. That energy can go into your energy body through the skin and the chakras, and suddenly, you have a spike in cortisol, and you feel anxious too. This happens more often than people realize. People sensitive to other people's energy can take on their emotions and health issues because they are pulled into their low vibration.

I live in a house with my husband, my three children, and three animals. Our home is jam-packed with many different frequencies trying to compete with one another. Unfortunately, if we are not careful, lower frequencies can dominate the higher frequencies if we do not create boundaries. My husband and daughter have dominating energy fields that can completely shift the room's energy when they walk in. When my daughter has an episode of anger and lashes out, and I am tired and feeling depleted, it is effortless for me to become unsettled and lose my balance. She can bring me right down in frequency if I do not practice boundaries. I think this happens to people all the time when they suddenly take on another person's emotions. It is important to feel an emotion and try to discern if it is our own or something we have taken on.

There are easy ways to discern if an emotion you are carrying is yours or not. You can do a muscle test or use a pendulum to ask where the emotion is coming from, or you can trust your intuition and ask yourself. Whatever you feel immediately is right, don't second guess it. When you stop to pay attention, you might realize that your anger is not yours. When you look back on the day, you may recall your spouse coming home from work angry, and a short time later, you were angry. That is a clue that you took on your spouse's anger. It's easy to release emotions that aren't yours once you figure out they are not part of your authentic resonance.

Envisioning an energetic grid of protection

There are many ways to create boundaries. The most impactful way to create boundaries is to distance yourself from the toxic people in your life and to make a conscious effort to detach from their energy field. Another way is to create an intention to disconnect from any energy not serving your highest good, from anywhere or anything, in all dimensions of time and space. In my previous books, I have shared many techniques on shielding and protecting yourself by creating golden bubbles of light around your auric field, surrounding yourself with the violet flame, and calling on your angels and animal spirits. However, there are a few other ways I have learned how to protect ourselves from psychic attacks and more effective ways to create a safe space around our auric field.

Protecting yourself using your own life force energy

Many spiritual teachers will guide people in protecting themselves by calling upon a higher being or light to protect them. I learned from an Arcturian in one of my healing sessions for a child that utilizing our light is even more powerful. I will share how the Arcturian showed me how to teach people to protect themselves from psychic attacks, shadow beings, and situations with a lot of 3D interference. He explained how children can use this method to expand their energy field to protect themselves in school or if they sense bad entities around them.

Stand with both feet on the ground and your hands beside you. Close your eyes. Take a few deep breaths through your nose to relax the mind and body. Next, envision your life force energy as a ball of light right in the center of your abdomen. Visualize this light as shades of gold and white. Connect to this light as your source of power that ignites your soul and connects you to the universe. Slowly visualize this light expanding into a larger sphere. A little at a time, your light is illuminating, expanding, and becoming more powerful. The sphere fills your abdomen and chest completely, and it begins to expand outside of your body. Feel the light becoming larger and larger until your entire body is within it. Feel it getting even bigger until it expands outwards, four to six feet in radius around your auric field. Take a moment while you saturate yourself with your own light. Take note of how you feel while embraced within your light bubble. Set the intention that this powerful light protects you and that anything and everything that does not match this frequency cannot penetrate through. You invite only the highest vibrational energy and entities for your highest good to merge with your light field. Open your eyes and go about your day feeling uplifted, empowered, and protected. You can check in with your light throughout the day to reinforce it by quickly tuning in and imagining the light is still shining brightly, and you are protected within it.

I take it one step further with children if shadow beings heavily attack them. Once they reach the step where their light is four to six feet outside their auric field, I have them visualize their light taking shape. I tell them to visualize a crystal with jagged edges in all directions. These sharp and pointy edges reinforce the protection around them so that the shadow beings will not want to come near them. I have heard back from many families that have tried this, and it has worked for many children. Of course, this can work for adults too.

Creating a Protective Grid

Imagining a bubble of light around your body and energy field can be very powerful. I have been using that method for almost 20 years. However, I have learned another powerful method of protecting our energy field. This visualization came to me during a session with a Lyran being. I was told to use this method to enhance our protective shield from other people's energy influence. I think this is a powerful method to use right now because there is so much division and turmoil among families and friends, and people are struggling to keep themselves calm and balanced. Many people are told to create boundaries, but most don't know how. Here is a simple way that a Lyran ambassador showed me. You can do this sitting, standing, lying down, or out in nature.

Close your eyes. Hold the intention to connect to your own energy source and life force. Visualize a strong energetic light coming down from right above your head that connects you to your Soul. This light can appear in any color, so allow it to occur naturally. Once you have established a direct connection to your higher self, try to connect to your light body by feeling the energy around your body. It might feel like tingles or buzzing. You may even see more colors. The light can be moving around in a pattern, a spiral, or creating a toroidal field. However it appears, try to connect to it. Then, visualize a portion of this light beginning to form a sphere around you with a solid border. Then, visualize the border of the sphere taking the shape of an intricate geometrical pattern. You don't have to have a conscious design of the pattern; trust that your subconscious will know precisely what you need. Place the intention that you are creating a grid of protection, utilizing your own light that is unique to you, and nothing can hack it or penetrate through it that is not in alignment with your highest good.

Boundaries are crucial, especially moving forward. I strongly encourage you to be more mindful about who you invite into your life. Who we surround ourselves with can either drain our energy and bring us down, or it can raise us up. It's all about energy exchange. Things are escalating at this point in the ascension, and many people must choose what direction to go. If you are choosing a path to become a better version of yourself, every decision you make is going to either reinforce that intention or cause setbacks. It is critical to create a strong system of boundaries so that you are in control of your destiny. The dark players can create 3D interference and 3D influence to knock us off balance, but if we stand firm in our light, none of their tactics will work. Boundaries are a line of defense; if they are strong, it is much harder to infiltrate our consciousness.

RELEASING BLOCKAGES

When we experience trauma, it is common for souls to dissociate. I have seen this a lot in my sessions, where a person will have endured trauma during childhood, and as a result, they dissociate. This is a survival technique of the soul so that it doesn't have to experience the full depths of the trauma, especially when it is outside of its control. I have also seen a large percentage of my clients who are newer Starseeds in their teens and twenties who have struggled throughout their childhood to fit into the 3D construct; therefore, their soul disconnects to the point where they have almost checked out. That is a dangerous position for our bodies because it leaves a void to be filled by wandering entities. Regardless of how or why the dissociation occurs, the impact is that the emotional process is severely limited.

Because of epigenetics, our DNA has shifted throughout the past generations, and people can more easily suppress emotions to adapt to a society built upon a *go-go-go* mentality. Whether to keep up with financial demands, peer pressures, or a distraction mechanism to deflect trauma, emotions are buried deep within the subconscious. The problem is that they become trapped within the physical and energy bodies and become stored as information. Despite what many believe, no scientific evidence supports the brain's ability to store information. So where does all the information go? I have been shown that the information is stored as energetic sequences and split between the physical and the non-physical. In the physical sense, energy is stored within the cerebral spinal fluid, the organs, the blood, the fascia, the bones, the teeth, the skin, the muscles, and on a microscopic level in every living cell.

On a metaphysical level, the energy is stored within all the layers of the light body, with a large percentage stored within the etherical blueprint. The emotions become trapped in both aspects because they cannot be released. When there are a lot of trapped emotions, the body becomes denser because there isn't a healthy flow of energy or *chi* within the body. The chakras are unable to function properly and blocks occur.

Discovering the root cause of dis-ease, dissociation, and emotional regression is the most profound pathway to soul healing. It takes mindfulness and patience to bring to the surface of our awareness the trail of breadcrumbs that led to the blocks. Whether there is one underlying trauma, a series of traumas, or a severe sense of not belonging within the 3D, the release of the blocks still requires the same steps. I have found that these are the most powerful steps to remove blockages:

- Intention

- Breaking the cycle of generational loops

- Becoming the observer

Intention

Our intention is one of our most underrated superpowers. Creating intentions sends a clear message to the universe through energetic sequences directed by our thoughts. That energy is then sent out into the quantum field around us, where it is mirrored and sent back to us. That is how manifestation works. We send the instruction, give gratitude that it has already come to fruition, and then let it go. If we truly live within a holographic universe, our intention is the blueprint, or the codes, that facilitate the programs. We are the designers of our reality through our thoughts, mindsets, visions, and beliefs. I believe the dark players try to intercept that process by implanting suggestions so that we create what they want us to create. They don't want us to know that our intention is what gives us the ability to create. If they constantly implant suggestions in every facet of our reality with doom and gloom, savior complexes, limitations, and a sheeple mentality, we will undoubtedly discount our sovereign ability to use our intention to create a better reality for ourselves.

I recommend setting intentions daily. Suppose we create new patterns with the innate knowing that our intention sets the tone for everything within our existence. In that case, we will realize how much control we have over the experiences we attract. Affirmations are a method of setting intentions. One of the easiest affirmations to say daily is, "*I am so grateful that I only attract experiences, relationships, and energy into my life that are in alignment with my highest good.*" Try saying this daily and see how your mindset, the types of people you attract, and your experiences shift. You may notice that the blocks you once perceived were driven by limiting beliefs, resistance, and fear.

I have had a lot of clients come to me because they are tired of being sick, being in abusive relationships, or living in poverty. Many of them have had similar stories where they say that drama follows them, and no matter how hard they try, they can't escape. The common denominator in many of these clients has been their resistance to change. They desire a better life; however, they are afraid to step out of the comforts of their current circumstance. They have so many emotions bottled up inside they can't breathe. They are so riddled with negative thoughts that some will argue with me when I try to tell them that their soul is in the process of learning something important. Until they pay attention, they will remain in that frequency.

Despite the high levels of 3D influence and 3D interference within our reality, I believe we all have the potential to become immune to it. I am already seeing this with new Earth children where the interference is not working on them as in previous generations. I believe the dark players know this, which is why they are pushing the transhumanism agenda at hyper-speed. It will slowly push out the soul if they can steal humankind by merging AI into the human body. It's as if the dark players are trying to initiate their own process of dissociation; although, their version benefits them because they can eventually possess ultimate control.

I have noticed a trend within the clients I work with who have the most difficulty navigating their awakening, where an awareness emerging from their subconscious triggers an innate knowing that they are within an illusion. They feel a deep surge of energy awakening them from a place they have never felt before. They are tuned into this feeling but are also paralyzed because of it. They have become cemented between their old life and the potential for something greater. This is because they have reached a new territory that life has not prepared them for. They didn't learn this in school. Their parents didn't teach them about this. Their church did not prepare them for this. They don't even know what *this* is because it's never been taught to them before.

Breaking the Cycle of Generational Loops

Activating and awakening can be a disconcerting process if you don't innerstand what is happening or have the bandwidth to lean into the process. So many people have been told throughout their life that they do not deserve anything more, so they become complacent and give consent to that frequency of existence. Through epigenetics, our ancestors have passed on genocide, enslavement, and suppression through our DNA, which creates ancestral loops and generations of limiting beliefs. There are layers of collective suppression and trauma, which is why it is so difficult for humanity to break free of the cycle. Generational loops are embedded deep within the blueprints of society, making them even more challenging to overcome. That is why so many people awaken simultaneously to generate waves of change. Each severed generational loop escalates the process for someone else as it gains momentum.

In 2024, I believe humanity is in the process of a mass awakening where cycles are breaking, limiting beliefs are being tested, and new thought patterns are being created. On a macro scale, the soul healing and awakening trajectory is imminent. On a micro scale, it is up to us to take back control of our sovereignty, and it begins with our intention and what we are putting our energy towards.

Becoming the Observer

There is one method I have found throughout my soul healing that has worked for me time and time again. I have placed myself in the position of the observer. When you take emotion out of an experience, you are left with an objective observation. Not to discount the emotional experience because it is the driving force behind many decisions we make in our lives. However, we have to know when to take emotion out of the equation to make decisions from a neutral perspective. If a person suffers from energetic and emotionally charged blockages, it will benefit them to remove the emotion so that they can take a step back to analyze the elements of the block. Simply by taking this step, profound discoveries can be made as you trace your steps backward.

There is a popular saying that *hindsight is 20-20*. I resonate with that saying because often when we look back at an event, absent of emotions, we see things more clearly. When we have had the chance to reflect, we can see the potential for alternative choices. That being said, in many cases, we learn valuable lessons from the mistakes we make. This creates a conundrum which creates the argument: *Do mistakes really exist?* I guess it depends on how you look at it. Either way, we have the power to pivot our lives at any point by stopping for a moment to reflect on whether or not we have blocks and what we can do differently to shift the energy. Sometimes, it's about asking the question and bringing your attention to your perceived blocks from a neutral perspective. By becoming the observer, you can perceive much more information than you would from a limited vantage point.

Reinforcing the Release Process

Once you establish the blocks, you can work to reinforce the release process. There are numerous ways to release. The techniques for releasing trapped emotions, limiting beliefs, and negative implants are too numerous to list; however, I will list the most common:

- Progressive and mindful breathing

- Meditation

- Mindfulness

- Reiki

- Regressive hypnosis

- Micro-dosing

- Emotional Freedom Technique

- Cranial Sacral Therapy

- Sound Healing

- Red Light therapy

- Salt Therapy

- Quantum Biofeedback

- Emotion Coding

- Access Bars

- Mindful and/or automatic writing

- Ayahuasca

- Spiritual therapy

- Mindful Exercise

CUTTING NEGATIVE CORDS

Energy cords are a natural part of our physical reality. Every interaction we have with someone has the potential to create an energetic connection. Throughout our lives, we develop energy cords with the people in our lives. These cords are like energetic pathways that create important connections that are necessary for the collective to grow and experience together. For example, a mother has an energetic connection to her child that starts with a physical umbilical cord. Once that cord is severed, an energetic line between them remains. That is why a baby will cry when their mom leaves the room, even if they don't see them walk away. The baby has an internal alarm system that goes off when their energy field recognizes that their mom's energy field has moved too far away from them. It's as if the energy cord between them becomes too thin, and there is an immediate energetic reaction. Now, we expand that example to the rest of the family. That baby also has energetic cords connecting them to their dad and any siblings in the home and even grandparents if they are close. Everyone has an energetic connection to the other members of their house. These energetic pathways crisscross and overlap. It can get confusing, but the idea is that every person on the planet has an abundance of cords connecting them to parents, friends, co-workers, mentors, teachers, romantic partners, children, siblings, and so on.

Most of the connections are positive until there are traumas. If a parent is abusive to a child, negative cords can develop between them. These cords can be tricky because they can cause strain in their relationship even if the abuse stops. The negative cords are like thorns on our sides; if triggered, they can cause a lot of pain and suffering. Most people unknowingly create negative cords throughout their lives as they experience negative relationships with people. These cords can occur for a lot of reasons, such as betrayal, obsession, grief, fear, abuse, neglect, and many other reasons. There are two main types of cords: active and passive. Active cords are generated when both parties are involved, contributing to the unhealthy exchange, whereas passive cords are one-sided.

Negative cords are unhealthy and can create havoc in a person's life. Cords can create blocks, and they can prevent people from being able to move on. The most common example of a negative connection with someone is when something occurs in the relationship that shifts the energy, and the connection is no longer in resonance with each other's highest good. In an ideal situation, the two people would walk away, wish each other their best, and not look back. Unfortunately, this is not a common occurrence in today's world. Instead, there is often resentment and pushback from one or both parties. Drama is created, sides are taken from others involved, and the negative energy between the people only intensifies. In this case, neither party can move on, and it causes dense energy to accumulate in other aspects of their life. That is because there is a constant pull into a lower frequency generated by the negative connection between the two people. If this is not resolved, it creates a more significant nuisance than either party intended, as it amplifies and affects their family and friends.

I first learned about cord cutting when I trained in Shamanic healing. It is very common in indigenous cultures throughout the world to participate in cord cutting practices. They believe that energy needs to be cleared between people so it doesn't become toxic. If there is a negative cord between two people, it can make it very difficult to move on. In situations where there are passive cords, it can hinder a person from moving on. Let's say a person leaves their abusive partner. This person has been with the abusive partner for many years, and they have been afraid to leave them because they feared for their life. When they finally leave them, they decide to cut them off completely, and they disappear. They can spend years trying to move on, but unbeknownst to them, they are still connected to that person energetically through cords. They may be trying to move on, but they are having nightmares, negative thoughts, unresolved fears, and a general uneasiness. This could be occurring because the abusive partner is still angry, they left, and they are still consciously connecting to the person, which is sending a signal through the cord to the other person's consciousness.

The person perceives negative energy transmission from their ex-partner as irrational thoughts and fears. They may be having trouble trusting another partner, and the negative energy being sent to them is inadvertently causing them hardship. The ex-partner may not have a conscious knowing that they are doing this, but if they are unable to move on and are angry at the person for leaving them, they can create this negative, unhealthy, and unresolved cord between them. Whether these negative cords are formed on purpose or not, nobody wins. Even when someone is unknowingly sending another person negative energy through their thoughts, it also negatively affects them.

That is why I am such a proponent of forgiveness. It is essential to free yourself from old contracts and negative energy from people in your life because if you don't, you are not going to be able to move on. You might think you have moved on, but what you don't realize is that there could be a tiny thorn in your side that is dormant, and when it becomes activated, it can cause a lot of unresolved energy to surface. Perhaps someone says their name or something reminds you of them. You might not have thought of this person for years. Then suddenly, *BAM*, you are triggered. Now that thorn is active, throbbing, and causing unhealthy thoughts and feelings to emerge. This can really throw you off balance.

I am going to teach you a few easy methods to cut cords for yourself. These are easy practices that anyone can do. You can even cut cords for other people if you have their permission. It is important to note that you can't cut positive cords. You don't have to worry about inadvertently cutting positive connections to a person. It is not possible to sever positive cords between two people. Some cords are foundational; much like ligaments are to bones, they serve an essential role. Regardless of whether a mother and child remain connected later in life, they will always have a positive connection. The good thing about positive cords is that you don't need to do anything about them. They shouldn't be a thought when you are doing clearings because you are only trying to clear cords that aren't serving your highest good anymore.

Cord Cutting Process

Much like any metaphysical practice, it takes a lot of faith, intention, visualization, imagination, and surrendering to fully embrace the process of cord-cutting. If you believe it is going to work, then it will. The more you can relax ahead of time and eliminate distractions, the more you can shift into the right brain. The logical side of us will block tapping into our greater senses. Analytical people struggle with esoteric ideals because their logical mind needs to make sense of everything.

Regarding energy, psychic abilities, connecting to the higher self, and trusting your innate knowledge, the left brain can't intervene. Sometimes, things won't make sense or will feel too good to be true. Many people hit a crossroads when this occurs, and their ego stops them from moving further. The right brain is your imaginative, playful side that embraces the journey. It is expected to say to yourself,

"Am I making this up?" I recommend that when those thoughts come through your awareness, you just let them flow in and out. Surrendering judgment and expectation is a big part of the process regarding any metaphysical modality.

Protection is a significant element of spiritual hygiene, so when you are participating in a modality where you are tapping into another dimension or frequency, you protect yourself. You can call upon your guides, star family, and angels to protect you, but I think the most powerful method is to protect yourself with your light and with strong intentions so that anything you are doing, connecting to, and receiving guidance from aligns with your highest good only.

When you are cutting cords, you are going to use your hands and visualization. Visualize your hands as powerful light beams that can cut through any lower vibrational cord or frequency like a laser. You can also use a selenite knife or a butter knife. Shamans believe that you need to use something with a sharp point, like a machete, to cut the cords. They don't use their hands because they don't want the negative energy to transfer to their hands and attach to them. It is my belief that your intention is the most powerful part of your practice. If your intention is that your hands are powerful lasers that can cut through and transmute negative energy, then you can't absorb it. You can even place an intention that you have an energy shield over your hands like a glove that protects you from anything you touch. Include in your intention that anything you cut from yourself or another person will not attach to you, and the universe will transmute the energy for the collective's highest good. That way, you won't have random loose cords floating around for someone to pick up unknowingly.

I prefer not to use tools because I feel more empowered that I don't need anything outside of myself. However, whatever you choose is what is suitable for you. There is no right or wrong way to do anything.

Become the architect of your own healing and follow your intuition. There is no book that can teach you what you innately know. You can only be given recommendations and tools like I am doing in this book, but ultimately, you will know what works and what doesn't.

There are two methods I am going to share. The first is a general sweep. In this method, you are not focusing on where the cords are coming from or where they are on the body. Your intention is to cut any cords that are connected to you that are not aligned with your highest good.

General Sweep

Sweeping Another Person

It's easier to explain how to sweep someone else first so that you can visualize the process before trying this on yourself. Once you have protected yourself, take a moment to relax your body through breathing. Take deep breaths and release any tension in your body. The more grounded you are, the easier these techniques will come to you. Have them do the same. Next, set an intention such as, *"Any and all cords that are connected to (name) that are not serving their highest good, I cut them on their behalf."* Ask them to focus their intention on releasing cords that aren't serving them while you sweep. Stand in front of the person and place your hand about 12 inches from their body. Starting at the top of their head and put your hand out in a stiff position with all the fingers together. With conviction and confidence, imagine as though your hand has shifted into a powerful laser of light, and slowly pass your hand down the front of their body until you reach their feet. With that motion, you are cutting through any dense, low vibrational cords connected to them. Set the intention that the cords that have been cut will fall to the ground and disconnect fully and completely from the person. You can ask Mother Earth to absorb the cords as they fall to the ground. Next, do the same thing on the backside. After you finish both sides, visualize the person in a bubble of pink, green, or blue light to heal those energetic wounds on the body so they seal up.

Sweeping Illustration

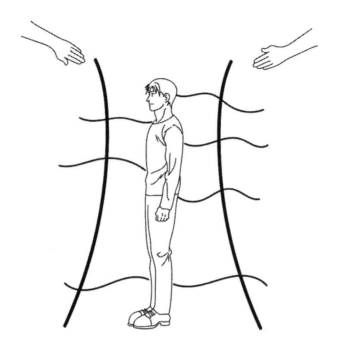

Sweeping Yourself

The process is the same when you sweep yourself. Relax, create your intention, and protect yourself. Stand with both feet flat on the floor, and using either hand, start above your head and sweep the front of your body, bending over as you get to your feet. Follow the same process of asking the cords to be transmuted into light or absorbed into the Earth. Next, you will want to do the backside. This part takes some imagination because we don't have arms on the back of our bodies. You are going to envision your back side merging with your front side. Close your eyes and visualize your back side is now facing forward. So, when you sweep your front again, you are actually sweeping the back. Try your best not to let your mind get the best of you in this step. It's easy to get hung up. It's natural for people to think overthink if they have to rely on faith that they are doing something that can't be seen. Trust in your ability, release doubt, and continue. After you finish both sides, visualize yourself in a bubble of pink, green, or blue light to heal those energetic wounds on the body so they seal up.

Negative Energy Cords

If you want to do an in-depth cord cutting, you can locate the cords on the body using your senses. This is an advanced method, but I believe anyone can do it. Begin by creating an intention that you are using your hands as a tool to detect negative cords in your own energy field or for someone else. This is one of those techniques where you really need to let go of reservations and feel into your knowing. Try not to overthink anything. Trust in your innate ability to track anything within the energy field that is not supposed to be there. Generally, cords will feel dense and disrupt the energy flow. They might appear in a specific color, such as brown, gray, black, or a dark hue. You may not be able to see or feel them, yet you will know one is present. Pay attention to all your senses. *What do you feel? What do you sense? What do you see? What do you know?* Trust your gut feelings.

I will share a brief protocol I have used for my own cord cuttings. Remember that this is just a guide; you can do it any way that feels right to you. There is no right or wrong way to do this technique. You can't hurt yourself or anyone in the process, but you can block yourself if you don't believe it will work. The first technique will be how to locate cords on someone else. The second will be how to locate cords on yourself.

Please note that whether you are cutting cords for yourself or someone else, you will not be able to cut all the cords in one session. State the intention that you are only cutting what is for the highest good of the person (or yourself). With any healing, the body needs time to process. You don't want to cut too much at once. You can do this weekly or whenever you feel intuitively guided. I wouldn't do this technique more than 2 to 3 times weekly. Once you are at a maintenance level where you feel like you have cut enough negative cords, once a month is probably enough. Unless you endure a traumatic event or feel like you have been around toxic people or you feel like something has attached, you can do this as frequently as you need throughout the year.

Locating Cords on Others

1. Stand about one foot in front of the person and put one of your hands (either hand) at the person's head. Close your eyes and begin to scan the body with all your senses. As you scan the body, pay attention to any shifts in energy and density. Lower vibrational energy will feel different than high vibrational energy. High vibrational energy feels light and airy, while lower vibrational energy feels cluttered and dense. Remember, you might not see or even feel the cord, but don't discount that feeling if you *sense* there is a cord.

2. When you find an area of the body that feels like there is an energy cord, use both hands and imagine as though there are either a bunch of tiny cords connecting to that area of the body or one thick cord. Pull them together with your hands like you would pull a bunch of rope together. It may take a few sweeps. Imagine as though you are pulling them together in one spot in front of you.

3. Hold the cord/cords in one of your hands, and with the other hand, using your selenite knife/butter knife/hand, visualize with the intention that you are cutting the cord by cutting through it. Place the hand that was holding the cords on the ground, asking Mother Earth to absorb the cords.

4. Go back to where you detached the cords and place your hand over the area, and with small clockwise circles, visualize that you are sending blue light to where the cord was cut. This will heal and seal the area where the cord was severed.

5. Scan the body for more cords (both front and back) and continue the process.

6. Once you are finished, ask them to ground. They can go outside in nature and immerse themself in fresh air, sunlight, and the light language of the environment (animal and nature sounds). If they are unable to go outside, have them stand up and visualize a beautiful golden light pouring down from the divine universe for their highest good. The light will travel through the top of their head and throughout their entire body. Tell them to remain in that energy for a few minutes so it can help them rejuvenate and rebalance.

Locating Energy Cords on Yourself

Locating cords on yourself is the same as finding them on others. You will follow the same steps. The only difference is you are guiding your hands in front of your own body until you feel something that needs to be removed. When you are ready to do the backside, set the intention that your back is coming to the front. This way, you can work on your front side, but you are energetically connecting the back of your body. Once you are finished, remember to visualize yourself immersed in a healing light and to ground yourself. This is a really important step that you don't want to forget. Think about it as a way to re-set after you have just purged a toxic amount of negative energy. You want to help your body by facilitating a wave of relaxation so you don't inadvertently go into a *fight-or-flight* response.

THE ENERGY BODY

The energy body, also called the light body or the auric field, is an essential aspect of our anatomical and physiological design. The physical body and the energy body communicate with each other every moment we are alive. You cannot affect one aspect without triggering the other. We should be taught about this in school; however, I believe it is discounted because the dark players don't want us to know about this side of our spiritual DNA. These subtle layers of energy that exist outside our body hold significant information. Each layer has a specific frequency that radiates in different colors. This is how auras are perceived. Some people have the ability to see the frequencies that surround and connect to a person. The aura can tell a lot about someone's mindset or state of being. This is why children and animals are so sensitive around certain people because they can sense these subtle energies. If someone has a low frequency, they will radiate a disconcerted energy, which can frighten children and animals.

It is important to be aware of our energy field and all its layers. There are seven main layers of the energy field and even more that exist beyond that. The closer the energy layer is to the body, the denser it is. As you move outward in layers, the energy becomes less dense and is much higher in frequency. Each layer shifts between yin and yang energy to promote overall balance within the energy body.

As health and wellness begin to move away from Western philosophies, I can envision energetic pathways to be included as an essential part of our educational health. This includes meridians, chakras, frequencies of colors and emotions, and learning about the energy body. All energy connects, and profound discoveries will be made if we are exposed to learning about the entire being and not limited to one aspect.

Illustration of the Energy Body

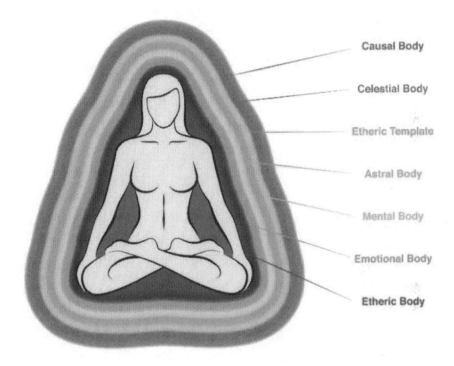

Causal Body

Celestial Body

Etheric Template

Astral Body

Mental Body

Emotional Body

Etheric Body

Subtle Layers of the Energy Body

Etheric Body

This is the layer closest to the body and it relates to our physical body and our health. It is connected to the root chakra. Guilt, shame, rage, fear, and ego can significantly affect the etheric body. This is where a lot of entities will attach to us. This is our closest connection to lower vibrational entities, lower dimensions, as well as the fourth dimension. If a person is working through a lot of traumas, it will reflect in the etheric body. I have learned that the majority of spells, hexes, cords, curses, implants, and viruses enter through the etheric body. I spoke in detail about etheric viruses in my previous book. I have seen many new Earth children get etheric viruses when they enter through the 3D birth portal. These viruses and low vibrational implants can work their way into the body through the root chakra.

Warrior spirits tend to have an active and expanded etheric body. Warrior spirits possess a strong will and desire to manifest change. They tend to be in the military or are athletes, and they are highly active. Because humanity has adopted a more sedentary lifestyle, the etherical body has become more restricted, allowing entity attachments and dis-ease.

The etheric space is our first connection to the tangible material world. Because of this, the etheric body is the densest. This energy field is intertwined and connected to the emotional and mental fields as they are always in communication. The etheric body is essential and foundational because it holds the physical matter of the body in place.

Emotional Body

This is the second layer of the energy field, and it relates to our emotions. This layer connects to the sacral chakra. This energy layer can show up on auric scans as many different colors, having a lot to do with the emotional state and balance of the person. It can expand and contract based on our emotional well-being. Our emotional body can extend 6 to 12 inches if we are happy and balanced. If we are in fear, worry, or shame, it is much closer to the body, roughly around 1 to 2 inches.

This is one of the layers animals will read when they meet a person. It is in the emotional and the mental body that allows them to discern whether a person is approachable. An intuitive person can tell a lot about someone when they connect with their emotional layer.

Mental Body

This is the third layer, representing our thoughts and our cognitive mind. The mental body connects to the solar plexus. It expands and contracts based on our thought process. If we are a creative person working on a project or a new business, this field can grow by 6-8 inches. If we are not in a creative mode and we are simply living life through routine and repetitive cycles, this layer can be 1-2 inches wide. It may also appear as a yellow hue on an auric scan. I believe this is where a lot of manifestation begins. We have an idea in our mind and we imagine what it would look like, and it builds energetically within the mental body. From there, it has the potential to expand to the higher layers of the energy body with a greater potential to become a reality.

Astral Body

This is the fourth layer, and it is the connective point between the physical body and the soul. This layer connects to the heart chakra. It's affected by our relationships with other physical beings. This layer connects us to our spiritual nature, and it serves as the pathway from the physical to the non-physical. The astral realm is very important right now because that is where a lot of this spiritual war is taking place. A lot of us travel to the astral realm during sleep and deep periods of relaxation, to fight off dark entities. It is from the astral space that souls are trapped within the void, so there is a lot of activity within the astral plane. In the astral space, people will interact with higher vibrational beings such as angels, fairies, spirit guides, and our star family. Beings can appear as orbs of light, energy patterns, colors, and in physical form.

The astral layer can be vibrant and bright when a person has loving connections with friends and family. When a person is going through a divorce or a harsh break-up, it can be dull and small. A person who meditates frequently, has lucid dreams, practices connecting to their higher self, and regularly disconnects from the 3D will have an astral layer 1 to 2 feet wide. It may appear as a hue of pink on an auric scan.

Etheric Template

This is the fifth layer, and it connects to the throat chakra. This layer is significant because it holds the spiritual blueprint of the soul. It also holds the physical blueprint of the current incarnation as well as others. This is where cellular memory is stored, so if you have a trauma in another timeline, it can be stored within the DNA. If that cellular memory is triggered, it can manifest in the current body. For example, if you had a severe back injury in another life, the cellular memory of the trauma is stored within the etheric template. If that aspect is triggered in this life through similar experiences that mimic the other trauma, the body will react by recreating the back injury. Many people have incarnated in this timeline to facilitate deep spiritual healing, not only for themselves but also for their ancestors. Because of this, the etheric template is very active in a large percentage of humanity.

Whatever you create in the physical will be stored in the etheric space. The blueprint for your life is represented as an energetic grid comprised of different frequencies and patterns. The etheric layer is connected to your ability to communicate well with others. A healthy throat chakra is a delicate balance of speaking your truth while respecting other people's boundaries. This can be difficult to do, which is why the etheric layer is very active and shifts frequently throughout your life.

Incarnating in a human form, navigating emotions, interpersonal relationships, and 3D interference is a difficult path. Our ability to discover our truth, live with integrity, and contribute to the collective awakening by being of service to others is how we activate our etheric template. It's called a template because we have the freedom to build upon our density of consciousness through experiences, reflection, and growth.

Celestial Body

This is the sixth layer, and it represents our wisdom and intuition. This energy layer is connected to the third eye chakra, which is the direct pathway to our higher self. When someone has an illuminated celestial body, their aura can appear bright white to silver. When a person has an innerstanding that we are all connected, they have a profound love for the universe and all life forms. They have the ability to remain neutral and are removed from judgement. Their density of consciousness is higher than most 3D humans, and they are here to guide humanity back to their sovereignty and innate knowing of their true powers. Celestial beings are selfless and do not operate in the ego. They are great mediators and prefer to stay out of conflict.

A person who is in their current life to heal and regain their empowerment will have a celestial body that is narrow and chalkier in color. Whereas, a person that is here to be of service to guide others through their healing will have an illuminated and expanding celestial field, expanding out several feet. New Earth children tend to have a very prominent celestial field.

Casual Body

The seventh layer connects to the crown chakra, and it is representative of our soul, our essence, and our life force. This layer is vibrant and strong when people are spiritually connected to their higher self, to God, and to the universe. The color of this layer can appear as a golden bright light. People who have a prominent casual body can appear to have a glow around them. Even people who can't see auras have the potential to see an active, casual body around someone. It's almost like the person is glowing.

It is very evident when you meet someone with an active casual body because you instantly feel safe with them. You feel like you can trust them without knowing them for long. They are humble, kind, and considerate of others. They are even known to give off an angelic presence. A person with an active casual body is multidimensional and has the ability to tap into more than one life at a time. They are active dreamers, instant manifestors, and are here to shift the trajectory of humanity. If you connect with this, you likely have an expanded casual body that others can feel and sense.

THE CHAKRAS

Chakras are the energy centers that exist in the etheric layer just outside the physical body. They are the gatekeepers of the energy that passes between the energy body and the physical body. There are seven major chakras that dictate this flow, and each chakra relates to a physical function of the body and to the emotions that match the vibration of each chakra. You can think of the chakras as the security system for the energy flow of the body. They control what energy comes in and out based on what is best for the body at the time. Chakras function like mini fans a few inches from the body. When they are working efficiently, they flow in a clockwise motion, allowing an appropriate amount of energy through them. When they are functioning at a lower capacity, they are either spinning clockwise yet very slow, or they reverse and spin counterclockwise. The flow can become disrupted by a negative emotional experience or an outside stimulus. The chakras can be affected by the environmental frequency or another person's energy merging with their own.

If a person doesn't know how to process and release emotions, whether theirs or not, they can become trapped. Trapped emotions can cause the energy flow to stop if it becomes too dense, which can cause a blockage in the corresponding chakra. The fan stops running when this occurs, and no energy flows in or out. Unfortunately, this is very common. A good majority of my clients have at least one chakra that is blocked due to past life events or traumas. There are many ways to clear and unblock chakras; however, it is important that the role of each chakra is understood. In the following pages, I will briefly describe the chakras and how they can be affected by environmental and emotional triggers.

The Chakras

Crown Chakra

Third Eye Chakra

Throat Chakra

Heart Chakra

Solar Plexus Chakra

Sacral Chakra

Root Chakra

Root Chakra

This chakra is located at the base of the spine. It is the foundation of where our body connects with the Earth and the world around us. This is a primal chakra where the life force energy fuels our survival. Our physical connection to our avatars resides here, along with our sense of stability and security, and whether we feel safe and supported. Our *fight-or-flight* and survival instincts thrive in this chakra. This chakra represents all that is physical. It is our tactile relationship with the world around us, what we see, touch, and the physical sensations of our bodies. If these experiences are positive, the chakra is open and flowing with ease. If we are put off by something, such as pain, it can close to protect the body. This is where doubt lives, and it is fueled by our deepest fears and regrets. This chakra flows smoothly and freely if we are grounded and balanced, feeling safe and supported. If we are scared, frustrated, or angry, it will disrupt the flow. The physical symptoms that follow can be hip pain, lower back pain, lower bowel issues, prostate enlargement, erectile dysfunction, sciatic nerve pain, and urinary tract issues.

Example of a Blocked Root Chakra

A person gets into an argument with their spouse. Voices are raised, heavy words are exchanged, and anger runs through them. The person leaves for work, and all day, the anger remains, and the person is unable to concentrate on work as she replays the argument in her head. The energy of anger is now in her emotional body just outside her physical body. As she remains angry, this energy will begin to flow through the root chakra and into her body. Her body reacts with an upset stomach, which leads to diarrhea. She returns home, doesn't speak to her husband, and goes to bed angry. Now, the energy of anger is positioned inside the body. In the morning, her root chakra may have slowed down significantly, causing her to wake up feeling un-well, nauseous, with more diarrhea. She now vibrates anger from her body out to the universe, and the universe responds by sending a similar energy frequency back to her. This can result in events that perpetuate the anger. Perhaps she gets a flat tire on the way to work; now, even more frustrated, she goes to work unsettled. Upon getting to work, she gets into an altercation with a coworker over something meaningless; however, in her state of mind, she thinks unclearly and takes it out on someone else. As a result, she now has the energy of frustration in her emotional body, which travels into a root chakra that has already slowed down.

As she continues her week in a low vibration, unable to release her anger and frustration, she gets terrible news over the phone, becomes overwhelmed, and breaks down in tears. With the compounding pressure on the root chakra, the result is that it becomes blocked as a defense mechanism so that no more energy can flow into the body. If this trajectory continues, the diarrhea could turn into acute irritable bowel disease. This may have been avoidable had she let go of the anger after the very first argument through mindful breathing, intention, and release work. Her frequency would have recalibrated and risen to a more balanced state.

Sacral Chakra

This chakra is located just below the navel, and it represents our sexuality and our artistic and creative expression. This chakra is more emotional than tactile. A significant aspect of this chakra is our intimate relationship with ourselves, how we feel about our physical appearance, our personality, our principles, and where we fit in the world impacts this chakra. This is also where our interpersonal relationships come into play. It's the aspect of our awareness where we consciously recognize there are other people in the world besides ourselves. Having meaningful relationships with others can create a positive flow of energy throughout this chakra.

Creative sparks and expressions are heightened and showcased through this chakra, where we feel free to broadcast our unique essence, personalities, and desires. If this chakra is not functioning to its true potential, we may lack artistic expression, creative drive, and the motivation to fulfill our purpose. We may become lost in traumas and lose our sense of purpose altogether. Negative experiences and relationships can impact this energy center, diminishing our ability to focus, which can stop us in our tracks. This can manifest physically as kidney infections or stones, digestive issues, lower spinal weakness, and female reproductive complications. If women are having difficulty becoming pregnant, it can be a result of a blocked sacral chakra. Their reproductive organs can shut down if their bodies perceive a threat or if it is not safe to procreate. If a woman is working through sexual abuse or even past life sexual trauma, her womb can shut down.

Our primal sexual drive resides in the sacral chakra. Because so many people in the collective have experienced some degree of sexual abuse, their sacral energy center needs healing. Anyone who is suffering from shame, guilt, low self-confidence, and low sense of self-worth, their sacral chakra will not function properly.

Example of a Blocked Sacral Chakra

Let's use the example of a long-term struggle with body image. This is a common cause of a re-occurring blocked sacral chakra. Many people have struggled with body image from a young age. As we develop and we are surrounded with other developing peers, it is natural to compare our bodies. Those who have struggled with their weight, for example, may create a negative body image growing up. Having felt uncomfortable and ashamed much of their adolescent life, they may grow up lacking self-love and confidence. This can create a chronically un-healthy sacral chakra. Perhaps as an adult, the person doesn't feel they deserve love, and as a defense mechanism, they put on more weight. Their body is receiving the signal that the more weight they put on, the safer they become. Their sacral chakra becomes blocked, and as a result, they suffer health issues like irritable bowel disease, diabetes, and lower back pain, and for women, uterine pain, endometriosis, and heavy periods. If this person worked on self-acceptance through mindfulness, spiritual therapy, release of trapped emotions, meditation, and a healthy diet, they would have an easier time healing the sacral energy. Having healthy relationships and boundaries is imperative for a healthy sacral chakra.

Solar Plexus Chakra

This chakra is located just under the sternum, above the belly button. This chakra represents our personal power; it's the halfway point of the primal human experience and the spiritual essence. This is an extremely important energy center because it brings together two worlds, the physical and the metaphysical. This is our emotional center, and much like a switchboard for an operating system, this chakra serves as the emotional epicenter. The energy that flows through a healthy solar plexus is confidence, empowerment, and that fire in the belly that ignites our passions.

Our solar plexus can operate as a warning system. If you have ever had a gut feeling about something, you were tapping into your solar plexus, which just so happens to correlate to the stomach. This chakra fuels and motivates the spirit to fulfill our life purpose. Most artistic people who draw or paint are tapping into the wisdom of their solar plexus, where creative sparks and expression manifest. If this chakra is not flowing well, you will feel anxiety and a lack of motivation. Some of the physical symptoms of a solar plexus that isn't flowing well are fatigue, stomachaches and ulcers, liver disease, and pancreatitis. When this energy center works optimally, you will feel like you can do anything you set your mind to. You will be filled with excitement, confidence, and empowerment.

Example of a Blocked Solar Plexus

A young adult embarks on his college career to become a physician. Since he was a young boy, he was groomed to become a doctor like his father and grandfather. He didn't want to become a doctor; however, he was never given a choice. He followed his family's wishes to follow the path of pre-med and then medical school. This young man is very artistic and loves to draw. In fact, he is an incredible artist. His teachers have encouraged him to continue drawing for most of his young adult life because he has a true gift. He often tried to share his passion for drawing with his father, yet he was never taken seriously. Over time, he shut off his creative side, not realizing that his life force energy dulled as a result. Over time, this closed off his solar plexus, becoming numb to what he truly wanted to do with his life.

In school, he developed chronic stomach aches, which led to ulcers and acid reflux. After many medical tests and pharmaceutical interventions, there was never any improvement. Energetically, what was happening was that the solar plexus became blocked and shut off the life force energy to that area of the body. As a result, there was acute stomach pain that led to a more serious chronic issue. As this young man continued to block off his *gut instinct* to follow his dreams, the dis-ease in his body became an issue that he could no longer ignore. If this person found the courage within himself to follow his passions, his solar plexus would begin to flow again, and his health issues would likely diminish over time.

Heart Chakra

This chakra is located in the middle of the chest at the level of the heart. It encompasses all aspects of love, whether that be love towards others or love towards yourself. When we experience hurtful moments in our lives, we sometimes place energetic walls or barriers around our hearts to protect us from getting hurt again. This could be one experience with a small barrier or many experiences with a wall so thick nothing is getting in or out. Our subconscious does all that it can to protect our heart, because despite what people believe, our heart is our most important organ. It feeds our energetic body and connects us to the universal consciousness. The electromagnetic field from our hearts is vast, and the subconscious protects it like the Secret Service protects the president.

Many clients who come to see me have a blocked heart chakra because they give out an abundance of love to everyone in their lives; however, they don't allow love into their hearts. They feel they don't deserve it, or their heart wall blocks love from entering. It is essential to love yourself and accept yourself first before you can love others in a healthy, more balanced way. In order for the heart chakra to flow appropriately, it must have a balanced flow of love. When it becomes unbalanced, it stalls and starts to spin counterclockwise, or it will stop flowing altogether. Some physical symptoms include heart flutters, arrhythmias, asthma, pneumonia, chest pain, and more severe, a heart attack. Make a point to analyze the flow of love in your life and how balanced it is. If you give out love yet don't allow it in or, tend to hold grudges and anger towards others, your heart chakra will likely become blocked.

Example of a Blocked Heart Chakra

We will use the example of a couple that recently ended their relationship. Let's say that the break-up was one-sided, and it left the other person entirely off guard and heartbroken. Filled with sadness, the person becomes depressed, starts eating poorly, and rarely leaves their home. They don't allow their friends' gestures of support to penetrate through their agony, so they remain in isolation. The person may begin to experience heart palpitations or an irregular heartbeat. They go to the doctor for an EKG, yet the results are normal. The doctor sends the person home with instructions to follow up if symptoms persist. Energetically, the heart has protected itself by slowing down the heart chakra – causing minor heart arrhythmias. If the person does not find the strength to forgive and move on, the heart chakra can become blocked, resulting in a more severe issue, such as a heart attack.

Conversely, if the person becomes motivated by their recent health scare to move on, they will be more likely to take better care of themselves. The choice to prioritize their wellness will raise their vibration, which may attract new people to enter their lives in a way that matches their frequency. Eventually, they will attract a partner that is in alignment with their highest good.

Throat Chakra

This chakra is located in the area of the esophagus and trachea, near the thyroid. The throat chakra is responsible for your ability to express yourself through words and verbal communication. If you are able to express yourself without fear of ridicule and judgment while maintaining awareness of how your words affect others, you will have a healthy throat chakra. If you have trouble saying what is on your mind or you hold back due to fear or worry of upsetting others, this chakra will be off balance. Humans have been given the gift of verbal communication, which can work in our favor and against us if used maliciously. Most galactic beings communicate telepathically or with sounds and tones, so there is little room for misinterpretation. In order for this chakra to flow appropriately, we need to follow our truth by voicing our opinions and expressing our uniqueness through the sound of our souls. If we hold back for too long, we can develop physical symptoms of acid reflux, coughing, tonsillitis, sore throat, and laryngitis. When we enable ourselves to talk to others respectfully while standing our ground, it gives us a sense of individuality. Communication is a valuable tool that can be complex and awkward at times; however, it can be incredibly satisfying, enriching, and an extraordinary gift.

Example of a Blocked Throat Chakra

In this example, we will use a shy, introverted young woman. Her entire childhood, she was told to speak when spoken to. She kept to herself in fear of getting into trouble. This fear became a way of life, and she kept to herself around her peers. Throughout her life, she became closed off and rarely spoke her mind. She became complacent and found herself going along with whatever her friends wanted, fearing upsetting them. Because of her long-term struggle with speaking her mind, her throat chakra was off balance most of the time, causing chronic strep throat. At some point, she felt strong enough about a specific issue that she spoke up, resulting in a confrontation with another person. Instead of standing her ground, she shut down and became frozen and unable to speak. As a result of this experience, her throat chakra became blocked. No longer able to function and out of protection, the chakra simply stopped flowing altogether. Over time, she developed hyperthyroidism, leading to a thyroidectomy.

This example is far too common, especially with women. Due to generations of suppression, women have a hard time speaking their minds, and subsequently, they develop thyroid conditions. Being able to speak your mind is a lifelong journey that should be taken cautiously and in phases. If people cannot speak their minds to their peers, family, and friends, they can start by expressing their feelings in other ways. They can start a journal where they write down their feelings. They can sing loudly in private to exercise the vocal cords and channel energy through them. They can express their feelings through fiction novels, art, and creating music. Eventually, they will practice expressing their truth to the people in their lives as they feel comfortable doing so. In the meantime, they must discover other ways to get their emotions out of the body so they don't cause a blockage leading to health issues.

Third Eye Chakra

This chakra is located between the eyebrows and it connects to our pineal gland. This chakra is the gateway to our higher self. When energy and the breath of life come through our nose, and through this chakra, our pineal gland opens. The pineal gland regulates melatonin and serotonin, the connection between the physical and the spiritual world. The more active the pineal gland, the easier we can connect to our intuition and our innate spiritual gifts. Many clairvoyants have an active and healthy third eye, assisting them in their connection with the divine and connecting to other people's higher selves. Suppose you have an active imagination, vivid future dreams, and a strong intuition. In that case, your third eye is likely flowing well.

If a person is plugged into the 3D and heavily programmed, their third eye will be blocked. Those people will be highly analytical, egocentric, materialistic, and likely to look outside themselves for guidance. They are not into spiritual practices, and they may even call esoteric practices demonic. When a person is medicated with antidepressants and anti-anxiety medications, they are blocking off their connection to their spirit. A person will not trust their intuition when the third eye is closed. They will require validation from their pastor, friends, and lovers. The physical symptoms of a third eye blockage range from ear, nose, and throat conditions to headaches, migraines, and eye conditions.

Example of a Blocked Third Eye

For this example, we will use a teenage boy and his spirituality. Let's say that this boy has always had a deep spiritual connection and belief in God, spirit guides, and angels. As a young boy, he remembered seeing beautiful angels in his room at night. They never scared him; if anything, they gave him a sense of peace and unconditional love. He was raised in a family that was not religious; however, he was taught to be a good person and kind to others. He grew up thinking that if he were a good person, he would attract the right people into his life and have a relatively peaceful life.

When he was 18, he was in a tragic car accident, and he lost his younger brother. He was so filled with grief that he turned his back on God and his spiritual beliefs because he could not understand why his brother was taken from him. He began to dissociate until he was barely living in the present moment, going through life numb and disconnected. In this example, his third eye was completely open until a traumatic event closed it off. Out of survival and cognitive dissonance, he shut off his spiritual side as grief took over. He turned his back on God, claiming that God would never allow an innocent child to die.

Unfortunately, this is common occurrence with grief, where the connection to the spirit becomes blocked due to disbelief as well as heartache. In this example, we can only hope that, in time, this person innerstands that everyone is on their journey. Even if we don't align with what they may have chosen before entering this life, we have to try to accept it. For many reasons, a soul may decide to live a short life ahead of time, whether for their karma or to teach those around them essential lessons. We may not ever know why a person decides to get ill, die young, or choose a life with many obstacles. However, we can try to be at peace with our soul's choices and not let them affect our journey.

Crown Chakra

This chakra is located just above the head and is our direct connection to Source. This is a powerful chakra that drives our universal life force, our connection to spirit and the Divine. This is the pathway to the collective consciousness of all life forms. Our awareness heightens when we open ourselves to the spirit realm beyond the physical aspect of our reality. The crown chakra integrates the whole being: the mind, body, and soul. This is the highest level of human expansion and our evolutionary process. This chakra will become blocked when we block our belief and openness that there is more to this world than our eyes can see. When we deny this aspect of our consciousness, a part of our soul lies dormant where it doesn't diminish or go away. Instead, it longs to blossom and be free. Physical symptoms of a blocked crown chakra are migraines, nervous system imbalances, fatigue, poor vision, and neurological issues. The emotional effects are depression, lack of desire, feeling disconnected, isolation, and difficulty connecting with others. When we elevate our consciousness, allowing us to connect to spirit, our galactic soul family, and Source, we raise our frequency to a point where we thrive and attract joy and abundance.

Example of a Blocked Crown Chakra

For this example, I would like to use a past client of mine. A woman came to me in her late 50s who suffered from chronic migraines. A friend recommended that she see an energy healer to see if reiki could help manage the severity of the symptoms. She came to me with an open mind and was open to talking about her life. I try to get as much background information as possible in my sessions. Because she was suffering from chronic migraines, I already knew she had a blocked crown chakra. I just needed to find out why. I asked her about her childhood, and she told me she was raised in a strict Catholic family and was forced to attend Sunday school with her siblings. As she spoke about her trauma of being raised in a strict Catholic family, it was clear how many unresolved emotions she had from her childhood. She explained how she never resonated with the religion. Because of this, she closed herself off entirely to God or anything remotely spiritual.

She recalled that when her migraines began, it was near the time when she moved out of her parent's home and chose to close the book on religion and anything close to it. She suffered from migraines for most of her adult life, and they became more severe as she got older. In our session, we discussed separating religion from spirit and how she felt about that. I did an energy session to open the crown chakra and balance the body. I sent her home with my first book, *Intuitive Transformation Evolution*. One week later, she called me back, eagerly looking for another session. She said that she finished the book, and something shifted in her, and she was happy to report she had not had any migraines that week. We set up several more sessions, and each time she would ask for a new book recommendation. After a month of working with her, her migraines did not return. She still reaches out occasionally to let me know how well she is doing and reports no migraines.

CHAKRA SPINNING

Chakra Spinning is a form of energy healing focused on opening the chakras. I learned about chakra spinning during a reiki session with a client many years ago. I saw a version of her in a past life where she was a powerful alchemist, and people would come to her to receive healing. I saw her opening and spinning people's chakras by manipulating them with her hands. A golden light came from her hand that connected to the chakra's energy center and would spin in a clockwise motion, creating a spiral. In that session, I could communicate with that version of her from that life. When I asked her what she was doing, she said, *"I am spinning the energy centers."* When she explained further, she showed me how she was manipulating the energy of the chakras to open them up. When I asked why, she explained that the chakras can become blocked due to grief, loss, illness, and travel. Like a person going to a doctor for a check-up, people would go to her to balance their chakras.

There are ways to balance and open the chakras that I have learned in my training, such as reiki, sound healing, and crystal healing; however, I had never heard of spinning the chakras before that day. She explained that it was an ancient technique and the most effective way to shift the chakras in her lifetime. She also explained that chakra spinning would make a comeback in future generations and that I would start offering classes to teach people how to do it. I was fascinated with chakra spinning after that session, and I remember researching it. Still, I was never able to find anything about it. It wasn't until years later that I decided to start offering chakra spinning classes at my wellness center in Bethesda, MD. I taught about two dozen people how to spin chakras, but then I began working with new Earth children, and I never taught the class again. I included this information in my book because it is the perfect time to resurface. Everyone should have access to this ancient technique of chakra spinning, regardless of whether or not I am teaching it.

How do Chakras Spin?

The chakras are energetic fans that allow energy to flow in and out of the body. When they are functioning normally, they spin in a clockwise direction. Our chakras function similarly if you think about a low, medium, and high-setting fan. A healthy chakra will function on a high-level flow. When there is disruption, the flow will shift and slow down to monitor what is coming through that shouldn't be there. For example, when a person experiences fear, the root chakra will slow down so the body doesn't become infiltrated by that frequency. Once the fear frequency has entered the body, it is up to the person to release it. There are many ways to release energy, such as mindful breathing, intention, reiki, and grounding, to name a few. The body will also release the fear through urine and sweat. The root chakra will flow appropriately once the frequency has been neutralized and the body returns to balance. Unfortunately, most people are not taught to do that as part of their spiritual hygiene routine, so the energy builds up in the body, eventually leading to a blockage.

Sometimes, the chakras can reverse and flow counterclockwise to self-correct. There are other theories about why the chakras flow in different directions, such as feminine and masculine influence. However, when I studied reiki, I came across so much conflicting information relating to the correlation of the flow as it pertained to masculine and feminine energy. Because of that, I had a difficult time resonating with the concept. Years later, when I had the session with the chakra-spinning client, I resonated deeply with what she said. That doesn't mean that there is only one truth; it just so happened that it was that truth that resonated with me the most. If I have learned anything on my spiritual journey, it has been to accept that there are many versions of the truth. Ultimately, you must trust your intuition and follow what you feel is right. I encourage anyone reading my chakra-spinning protocol to take it for what it is. If it resonates, then wonderful. If it doesn't, that's ok, too.

How to Spin the Chakras

You can assist the chakras by manipulating the energy flow by hand. The process works best when you combine the intention that you are releasing any blockages by increasing the energy flow of the chakras so that the trapped energy can be released. When you use reiki to clear the chakras, you channel universal life force energy through your body and the chakras to open them up. Chakra spinning does not channel life force energy or pull energy from the universe. Instead, the process is facilitated by a method of energetic manipulation using your intention and your direction. Once you connect with the chakra, you can guide the fan to move as you motion for the energy to spin. This might sound a little nutty, but I assure you, it is simple and effective. Remember to breathe and relax before attempting esoteric modalities. You can shift from the brain's left to right hemispheres. And remember not to over-think it.

How do I know if the chakras are spinning correctly?

You don't need to have a reason to work on the chakras or know how they are functioning to work on them. You can work on them daily to promote a healthy flow, which I call maintenance. However, if you know there is an area of the body that is bothering you, it is recommended that you work on the chakra most closely related to that ailment. For example, if you develop acute headaches with no apparent cause, such as dehydration or a new medication, you can try spinning your crown and third eye chakra. This brings me to my next point: more than one chakra can be affected at a time. You can refer to your chakra chart for more information on this.

Spinning Chakras for Others

Like in previous techniques, doing this exercise on others is easier. It's much easier to feel and move the chakras for someone else than it is for yourself. Once you get the hang of the process from practicing on another person, it will be easier for you to try on yourself. Of course, you will need permission to work on someone. Once you have their consent, you can explain to them that you are not going to touch their body and nothing you are doing can hurt them. You will want to keep a clear line of communication with them while you go through each chakra to check in with them. They may experience emotional release or a shift in breathing. You don't need to know anything about their personal life if they don't want to share with you any details of their intimate life ahead of time.

Set the intention that you are opening and clearing their chakras for their highest good only and that you are facilitating the release of only the energy and emotions they are ready to release. It is helpful if they create a similar intention in their mind that they are open to receiving the healing and that they are willing and ready to release anything that is not serving their highest good at that time. Set another layer of protection and intention by creating a visual, energetic grid around you so that no uninvited lower vibrational energy comes into your space.

Here is a chakra chart and flow illustration to guide you during your practice. Note that the crown and root chakras flow differently, so that the spinning process will differ slightly.

Chakras   ## Energy Flow

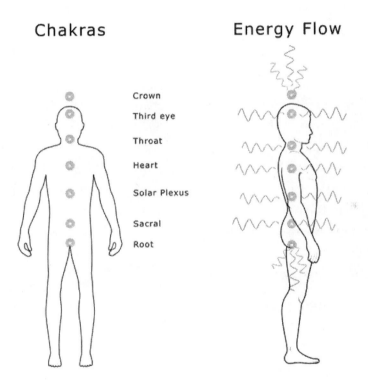

Crown

Third eye

Throat

Heart

Solar Plexus

Sacral

Root

Chakra Spinning Steps

1. Have the person stand comfortably with their hands at their sides, and their eyes closed.

2. Stand facing them and hold your hands so that the palms of your hands are facing each other. Start with your hands about 6 inches apart from each other, and slowly bring them together until you feel your own energy field. You can close your eyes if it helps. Slowly bring your hands together until you feel tingling, pulsing, buzzing, or similar sensations in your hands. If you don't feel anything, just trust that there is energy there, even if you can't feel it.

3. Starting with the lower chakras, locate the root chakra at the base of their spine. It will be positioned in the body's center, right around the groin, a few inches from it. Place your dominant hand about 6 to 8 inches in alignment with the root chakra in front of the body. The palm of your hand should be parallel to the body. Once you locate the chakra, you must shift your hand down about 45 degrees to align with the flow. The root chakra flows slightly down towards the ground. (You will have to bend down for this step.)

4. Take a moment to connect with the other person's root chakra by simply keeping your hand in the pathway of the energy flow. You might feel a gentle energy coming from it or a slight tingling in your hand. If you don't feel anything, that is ok. (Remember how your energy felt in comparison)

5. Turn your hand so that your fingers are pointing towards the chakra and start to move your hand in a clockwise motion at a 45-degree angle. Move your hand in small clockwise circles. This process will cause the energy from their chakra to align with your movement. Continue spinning for 15 to 30 seconds

in small circles, then slowly begin to increase the size of your circles as you slowly move back to approximately 12 inches from their body. Continue spinning for another 15 to 30 seconds, or until you feel intuitively to stop. Take your hand out of their energy field and note any emotions or visions you had while spinning that chakra. Ask the person if they felt anything during this process as well. They can have an emotional as well as a physical response.

6. Move on to the sacral chakra and start the process over. The only difference is that for the sacral, solar plexus, heart, and throat, you will spin straight outwards in alignment with the flow of those chakras. Spend roughly 45 seconds to 1 minute on each chakra before moving on. Take note of the difference in energy coming from the chakras before and after you spin them. Also, make sure to ask them how they are doing throughout the process.

7. Once you reach the crown chakra, it is helpful to have the person sit down so you can reach the top of their head. Place your hand about six inches above their head to locate their energy field. Once you feel connected, begin to spin your hands in a clockwise direction above their head and slowly make bigger circles as you move farther away. This step can make people feel dizzy, so it is a good idea to have them sit down.

A few important things to note. You don't need to spin the back side of the body because the chakras are connected on both sides. During this process, the person can lie on a massage table or couch, and you can work over them. Don't stop; even if you don't feel a lot of energy during the session. At least finish the process and let the person see if they notice a shift. They may not notice anything right away. That's because the body needs time to re-balance and integrate after any energy work. This can take time. How much time depends on the person. I have done spinning sessions for people in the past who felt overwhelming energy surges during the process. I have also had people say they felt nothing. Some people are more sensitive to energy than others. Regardless, I believe it works whether they feel something or not.

Whether you are spinning your own chakras, your children's, or someone else's, you can repeat the process as often as you need. It can be part of your daily routine or whenever you feel called to do it. This process is completely safe. It is a great way to ground children. I recommend when working with children that they lie down on their backs. This way, they will be able to stay still for longer. You can expedite the process for them because children process energy quickly. You can spin each chakra for about 30 seconds, half the time as an adult. Another helpful hint is to do this while they are sleeping so they are completely still and open to receiving. This practice is especially important if they suffer from anxiety or during periods when they are sick. Remember, colds and flus are not always a bad thing. They are our body's way of detoxing and releasing dense energy. The best thing we can do during those periods is rest and assist the process through grounding, reiki, chakra spinning, meditation, and taking natural supplements.

Spinning for Yourself

1. Take a moment to set an intention to release any energy holding you back from being your best self. Take a few deep breaths to calm the body down. Place yourself within a grid of protection.

2. Start with your hands about 6 inches apart from each other, and slowly bring them together until you feel your own energy field. You can close your eyes if it helps. Slowly bring your hands together until you feel tingling, pulsing, buzzing, or similar

sensations in your hands. If you don't feel anything, just trust that there is energy there, even if you can't feel it.

3. Starting with the lower chakras, locate the root chakra at the base of your spine. It will be positioned in the center of your body, right around the groin, a few inches from the body. Place your dominant hand about 6 to 8 inches in alignment with your root chakra. Once you locate the chakra, you will want to shift your hand down about 45 degrees to align with the flow.

4. Since you are working on yourself, you can position your hand in any way that feels natural. Once you feel ready, slowly spin your hand counter-clockwise at a 45-degree angle so that energy flows toward the ground. Continue spinning for 15 to 30 seconds in small counterclockwise circles, then slowly increase the size of your circles as you move your hand about 12 inches from your body. Continue spinning for another 15 to 30 seconds or until you feel intuitively to stop. When you are done, place your hands down to give yourself a moment to process before moving on. Take note of any emotions or visions you had while spinning that chakra.

5. Move on to the sacral chakra and start the process over. The only difference is that for the sacral, solar plexus, heart, and throat, you will spin straight outwards in alignment with the flow of those chakras. Spend roughly 45 seconds to 1 minute on each chakra before moving on. Please take note of the difference in energy coming from the chakras before and after you spin them.

6. Once you reach the crown chakra, place your hand six inches above your head to locate the energy field. Once you feel connected, spin your hands over your head counterclockwise.

Slowly make bigger circles as you move farther away. This step can be tiring for your arm, so do it for as long as you can. This step can make you feel dizzy, so it's a good idea to sit for this one.

Life Force Energy & Earth Grounding Technique

This is one of my favorite methods to ground and pull in high vibrational life force energy from the universe. This technique realigns the physical body with the energy of the Earth as well as the God Source frequency. This process is a unique and profound way to balance the mind, body, and spirit through mindful connections to both the Earth's frequency as well as the frequency of the collective consciousness. When you intentionally connect your body to the Earth's frequency, you facilitate rejuvenation, release, integration, and grounding. When you connect to the universal life force energy, you raise your frequency, bring in more light codes, and activate the soul.

This is an ancient technique passed down from the indigenous ancestors over generations. Many shamanic traditions use a similar balancing method by connecting to the physical and metaphysical energy lines. This process creates energy lines from both energetic frequencies and connects them to the major and minor chakras. This synergy promotes optimal energetic balance, unlike anything I have seen in other modalities. This is an easy technique that anyone can do. There are no rules, and I encourage you to add anything to the practice that enhances the outcome.

Please note that the process is the same whether you work on yourself or another person. I will list the steps for a standing position. However, you can do this exercise in other ways, such as in a relaxed, meditative state where you visualize the lines instead of physically drawing them out. I suggest you get used to this technique by physically going through the movements before you try doing this through visualization.

A Quick Note on Children

This is an excellent exercise for children. You can teach them to do this independently or you can pull the energy for them. They can lie down or stand up. This is excellent for children who are struggling to ground themselves. Since I work with many high-frequency children, I have noticed that their main issue is grounding to the body because they are often *floating* due to being so multidimensional. I created a hack for this exercise to assist children needing grounding. For every minor and major chakra, pull two lines of Earth energy and one line of source energy. This way, they are really anchoring into their body to ground and integrate by receiving a 2:1 ratio. Similar to chakra spinning, you can do this exercise while your children are sleeping to ensure they don't move around during the process.

The following is an illustration of the major and minor chakras. You will see the seven main chakras in the middle of the body and six minor chakras in the feet, knees, hips, hands, elbows, and shoulders.

Grounding and Universal Life Force Balancing

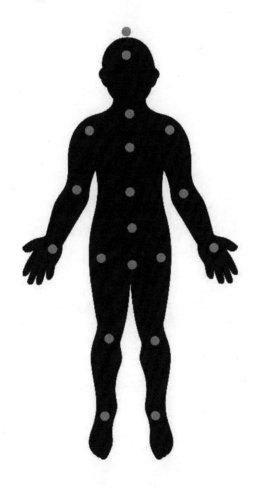

Life Force Energy & Earth Grounding Steps

1. Stand with two feet firmly on the ground. Barefoot and outside is best but not required. Take a moment to relax, breathe, and set an intention. Your intention can be, *"I connect myself at this time to the highest frequency of universal life force energy that is in alignment with my highest good as well as the healing and grounding frequency of Mother Gaia."*

2. Begin by using two hands, bending down to the ground, and visualizing as if there is Earth energy at your feet that you can grab with your hands. You can visualize this energy as the color green, but it's not necessary. Pretend as though the energy can be picked up with your hands, and as you bend down, you pull some of the energy up to create a cord or a line. It's as if you are pulling lines of Earth's energy from beneath your feet.

3. We will start with the minor chakras first. Pull this energy up using both hands just slightly until you reach the top of your feet. Then, you will drop the lines into your feet by placing your hands over your feet, symbolizing that you have attached that energy line from the Earth to the minor chakras in your feet.

4. Next, reach your hands up towards the sky and visualize that there is God's Source energy, or universal life force energy, above you that you can grab. I usually visualize this energy as bright white. Using both hands, pull two energy lines down from above and place them on your feet. You have created an equal amount of energy from above and below to harmonize and balance the feet chakras.

5. Next, do the same for all of the minor chakras (knees, hips, wrists, elbows, and shoulders). All of these areas will require two lines using two hands. The only caveat is when you get to your hand/wrist and elbow chakra, you will have to crisscross

the lines to the opposite arm since it's too difficult to place those lines in the same arm.

6. Now, it's time to move on to the major chakras. The difference is that you will only need one hand to pull energy lines since there is only one major chakra point. Starting at the root chakra, bring lines from Earth and Source, making your way up to the crown. All major and minor chakras will have equal lines from both frequencies. Once you are done, visualize the entire body illuminated in a bright white light to seal it in.

7. When you are done, bring your hands together and give thanks. Make a note of how you feel once you are finished. You may not notice a significant shift right away, but the more you do this exercise, the more you will feel an overall sense of well-being.

The following are illustrations to guide you as a reference for the different points as you work through the major and minor chakras.

Universal Life Force Energy

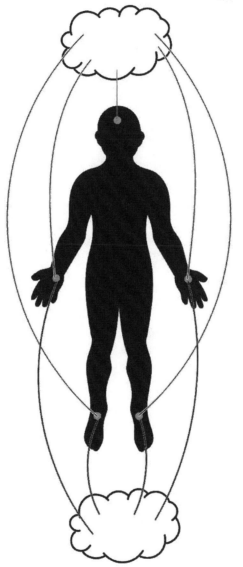

Earth Grounding Energy

7 Major Chakras

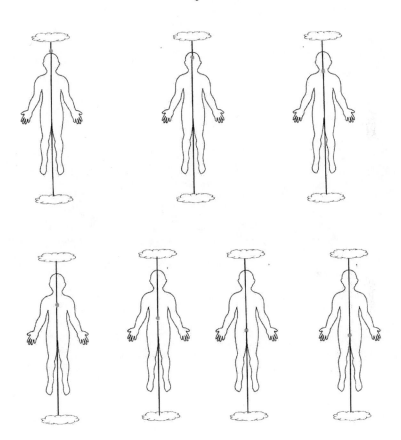

6 Minor Chakras

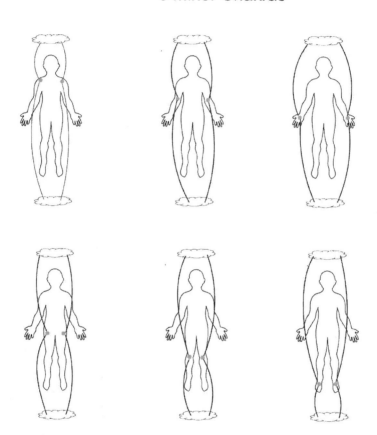

SOUL RETRIEVAL

Soul retrieval is an important aspect of any soul healing. When we experience a life with trauma, disease, or hardship, a fractal of the soul can break off and remain in the energy of that life, even when we have passed on. I first learned about this during my transpersonal hypnotherapy sessions in 2016. When I regressed someone into another lifetime where the trauma occurred, I could see that an aspect of their energy remained long after their soul exited that life. I began performing soul retrievals by calling upon the soul fragments to release themselves from that timeline and merge back with their soul.

A good way to describe this is by using the metaphor of a puzzle. The puzzle pieces break apart when the soul fractals out to live different lives. When that aspect of the soul returns from a life, the puzzle piece that represents that life, returns. If a soul endures trauma during a life, it can become fragmented, and that one puzzle piece can fractal into many smaller pieces. If there are many lives with trauma or disease, many small pieces of our puzzle become disconnected from us, leaving us looking like a large puzzle with random missing pieces. As a result, in our current life, we can feel as though we are not whole or pieces of us are missing. Even if this is occurring at a soul level, we can still perceive this through irrational thoughts, lack of desire, and depression. More severe symptoms can cause split personality disorder or bipolar disorder.

I have seen a positive impact on people who have done soul retrievals and those who implement the soul retrieval process once a year. This is a simple yet profound process that can bring up emotions buried deep within the subconscious, so I recommend that before trying this exercise, you take the time to try some of the other techniques I have laid out in this book first. There is a reason I put this last because it can be the catalyst for profound discoveries, epiphanies, and activations. Lastly, your expectations should be limited to what your soul is ready for at the time you perform the soul retrieval. Our bodies have to transmute and process any healings that we perform. You don't want to overload the body with too much to process if it can't handle it. The good news is that if you set an intention to call in the fragmented aspects of your soul that are in your highest interest only, you don't have to guess. Your intention is the most powerful part of this exercise.

Soul Retrieval Process

1. Relax the body through meditation or mindful breathing. Set an intention that you are calling upon the fragmented pieces of your soul that have become lost, trapped, or disconnected and are ready to return.

2. Protect yourself with your own grid of light. You can call upon your guardian angels as well.

3. In your mind, make a general statement such as *"I call upon the lost, trapped, and disconnected pieces of my soul to me at this time. I call upon you with endless love and compassion, and I apologize for any trauma you have been through. It is safe to rejoin me now; as we travel into a higher state of awareness, we evolve together in harmony and peace."*

4. Close your eyes and visualize yourself standing at the top of a very high mountain, looking out into the infinite space beyond your dimensional reality. Visualize those pieces of you beginning to reveal themselves. At first, this may look like tiny

specs of light that appear all around you. You may see only a few or too many to count.

5. Now imagine as though those tiny specs of light merge with your body as you become one. Instead of a mountain, you can visualize yourself anywhere you feel safe. You can be a large tree; the soul fragments are leaves returning to the branches. You can visualize yourself as a flower, with petals returning to create a bigger flower. You can visualize yourself as a mason jar and tiny fireflies come back into the jar. You can visualize yourself as a bright, shining star, and the smaller stars around you merge with you to create one large star. Allow your imagination to create whatever you need to facilitate the return of your lost fractals of light.

6. Allow yourself to sit and receive this energy as you become whole again. You may become emotional during this experience. I recommend allowing emotions to flow. Cry if you need to. Scream if you need to. Jump up and down if you need to - whatever helps you integrate and receive the energy that is right for you. When you are done, give thanks and bring yourself back to the present moment. Have faith that whatever aspect of your soul that was ready to return, did so without hesitation. Allow yourself time to integrate this level of healing before trying this exercise again. I recommend waiting at least a week in between sessions.

MEDITATIONS

I have written the following guided meditations to assist you in different ways. The idea is that you read the meditation, then go to a comfortable space, close your eyes, and follow my guidelines. Feel free to change any details and customize it to your liking.

Meditation to Connect with Your Higher Self

After a few moments of progressive breathing, visualize yourself in a large meadow of lush green grass. Feel the warm summer breeze as it gently caresses your face. Look up into the sky at all the beautiful white fluffy clouds. Watch as one of the clouds descend from the sky and into the meadow at your feet. Allow yourself to get onto the cloud and lay back comfortably, as this special cloud can hold your weight. Make the Intention to leave your conscious mind to rest in the safe space of the meadow below. Allow yourself to rise with the cloud back up in the sky --- slowly and freely, feel yourself rise. With every breath you exhale, you feel lighter and more relaxed. Allow the cloud to rise higher in the sky until you can no longer see the meadow below. As you continue to float higher, you reach a marble platform with columns on either side. Allow yourself to get off the cloud and onto the platform. Visualize an Angel or a guide greeting you on this platform, which will accompany you down the walkway to your higher self.

As you continue down the walkway, you reach a special door that can appear any way you wish. This door leads to your own very special room where you can speak with your higher self, the part of you that stores the wisdom and knowledge of your Soul. When you are ready, open the door and allow your imagination to reveal to you what your unique room looks like. You will likely be greeted with a mirror image of yourself with slight variations. Imagine walking over and greeting this three-dimensional version of yourself and pausing to see if there are any messages, feelings, or images that come to mind. Next, ask for guidance on a particular issue, and be patient while waiting for a response. It may come as flashes of images, words, thoughts, or emotions. Just let it flow without judgement. Lastly, imagine a beautiful pink light flowing back and forth between the two versions of yourself from the base of the heart. This pink light represents self-love and care. Allow it to flow with ease for a few moments as it rejuvenates your body and soul. Once you are ready to leave, return down the walkway until you reach your cloud. Lay down on the cloud and visualize yourself descending back into the meadow. Once you get back on your feet, allow yourself to be grounded by remaining on the grass for a few seconds before opening your eyes.

Grounding

If you can do this meditation barefoot on the grass, it will be more impactful. However, if that is not possible, you can do it in your home with your feet firmly on the floor.

Take a few progressive breaths to help relax your mind and body. Stand with your arms beside you, loose and limp, and both feet on the ground. You can close your eyes or keep them open if you are worried about losing your balance. Then simply, ask Mother Gaia if she can assist in grounding you by rejuvenating you with the frequency of Gaia. Visualize the core of the Earth opening up as a brilliant white light cracking open like an egg. As the light pierces through, it travels up the layers of the Earth, through the ground beneath you, and up through your body until it goes out through your head or Crown chakra. As the light travels through your body, it revitalizes the body and soul, energizing and uplifting your vibration, grounding your body while connecting your soul to Source as it exits through your Crown. Once the energy stops flowing (only a few minutes is necessary), thank Mother Gaia for her beautiful gift.

Angels Release

This meditation is for those who are more spiritually inclined and prefer the assistance of an Angelic presence. Start by doing a few minutes of progressive breathing and ask to be surrounded by protection while you do this meditation. Ask your angels to be present before you begin to ensure they are permitted to assist you. Ask for the highest vibrating Angels to help in your healing and eliminate any chance of lower energies interfering.

Proceed by visualizing yourself walking into a beautiful dome of divine light that is a vibrant gold or white. Allow yourself to walk through the energetic barrier until you are inside the dome. Once you are inside, an Angel greets you. If you can't visualize an Angel with a physical body, just feel their presence. The Angel will come close to you and open your crown chakra just above your head with her hands. Ask her to assist in the release of any negative energy and trapped emotions in your body at that time. Feel her begin to pull the energy out of your body through your head, as though her hands are a vacuum, pulling out energetic blockages from your body. You can contribute by asking for specific energy to be released, or simply trust that whatever is not serving you is being released.

You can stay within the dome of light for as long as it takes until you feel the pulling stop or until she closes your crown and steps back to let you know the clearing has been completed. Next, imagine that the dome you are in suddenly becomes illuminated in golden healing light. Allow your body to be saturated by this beautiful healing light as it flows through and around your body, filling the spaces you just released with a rejuvenating, powerful, all-encompassing light from the universe. Stay in this light as long as you need to. When you are ready to leave, go through the dome until you are outside of it, and open your eyes.

Hot Air Balloon Release

Start by doing a few minutes of progressive breathing and ask to be surrounded by protection while you do this meditation. Visualize a beautiful large hot air balloon in front of you. Imagine all of the colors and designs of your balloon. Allow yourself to get into the basket. Once you are inside, it begins to rise. You travel over beautiful mountains and valleys or whatever comes to mind. You look down and notice that there is a box on the floor of your basket. Open the chest and place inside all the emotions, events, fears, and anxieties you want to release. When you are done filling the box, close the lid and imagine you are now over the ocean, traveling low enough that you are not far from the ocean surface. When you are ready to release the emotions, pick up the box and toss it over the basket and into the ocean. The ocean is a beautiful turquoise, and you can see through the water below. Watch as the box sinks. The ripples of water at the surface carry away emotional residue, and your box sinks to the ocean floor. Immediately, you feel the balloon rise slowly up high in the sky as the weight of those emotions being released allows you to rise, elevating you to a place of clarity and peace. Stay floating in your balloon as long as you wish, saturating yourself in this newly found freedom and calm.

Forgiveness

Imagine yourself in a beautiful healing room after a few minutes of progressive breathing. It can appear any way you desire with beautiful lights, angels, flowers, the moon, and stars - whatever comes to mind. Then, visualize yourself standing in that healing room with the person you are forgiving standing facing you. Next, think about that person as a soul, not just as the body they are inhabiting. They may have a beautiful aura around them. They may shift in some way to reveal their true essence. Take a moment to tell the person how they hurt you, allowing all the emotions to come forward. Then, visualize an energetic cord connecting the two of you. This is an unhealthy, negative cord filled with all the emotions associated with your connection. Next, tell the person that you forgive them for hurting you because you understand that it came from a place of weakness, and you know that their soul is pure and good, regardless of what they did to you. Tell them that you are choosing to cut the cord between you, disconnecting you from this pain they have caused you, to free both of you once and for all. Next, imagine a powerful white light, almost like a lightsaber, cutting through the cord and severing it completely. When the cord is cut, visualize it dissolving into the white light. Once you no longer see the cord. Imagine a beautiful pink light surrounding your body, sending you love, peace, and calm. Watch as the pink light spreads over the other person, giving them the love and soul healing they need. When you have received enough of the pink light, say goodbye to the other person and watch as they disappear. Once they are gone, thank the universe for assisting in this healing, and open your eyes when you are ready.

Cleansing Shower Meditation

This is one of my favorite meditations, and you can do it every morning or evening. When you are in the shower, imagine the warm water running over your body, clearing your aura of all unwanted and negative junk. This is a simple meditation that relaxes the body and mind. In your mind, ask that the water cleanse and purify your energetic body back to balance, and ask that all energy attached to you that is not of your highest good be washed away and taken down the drain. Allow yourself to relax, loosening any tension in your body as the water flows. Set your intention to release, release, and release.

Waterfall of Colors

This meditation is one that I frequently share with my clients when they come to me for an energy session. It is a simple way to cleanse the Aura of unwanted energy using colors. This meditation should be done in a comfortable position. A few minutes of progressive breathing can be done first to relax the body.

Close your eyes and visualize that you are in a beautiful forest: imagine the trees, the ground beneath you, the sounds of birds in the distance, whatever your imagination reveals. Visualize walking towards a beautiful waterfall flowing into a body of water below; only this waterfall is full of bright colors. All the colors of the rainbow are flowing down the waterfall. You can walk on a ledge that takes you right under this waterfall of colors. Once you visualize yourself standing under this waterfall, visualize that, as the colors wash over you, they are cleansing your Aura of all unwanted energy. As the colors flow, allow yourself to release and relax. Once you have spent enough time under the waterfall, when you feel Intuitively that you are done (3-5 minutes), walk away from the waterfall. Now, visualize a beacon of golden light coming down from the sky between an opening of trees a few steps away. Stand under that golden light and energize yourself by the Universal Light. Ask that it replenish you and surround your entire energetic body, giving you a boost of love and light.

Powerful Magnet

I like to use this method to visualize the energy within my body that is not serving my highest good to be pulled up by a powerful magnet. I follow it up with a brief shower of light to fill my body with rejuvenating light.

Close your eyes and visualize yourself in a beautiful forest under a canopy of trees. There is one spot above your head where the canopy of branches opens, and the sun is shining through. Take a moment to connect to this space and ground to the Earth. Next, visualize a metallic disc about 1 foot in diameter floating about 1 foot above your head. State the intention that this disc can pull only low vibrational energy within your body and the light body that is not serving your highest good. Feel as though the disc is starting to pull denseness from the body like a vacuum. Visualizing any negative cords, negative energy, trapped emotions, implants, entities, or anything that is lowering your vibration, being pulled up and out of your body and into the disc. Do this exercise for several minutes and feel how your body reacts to the energy's movement. Do not resist the urge to cry, scream, shake your body, or do anything that can assist the process. Once you feel intuitively that you have removed all you are capable of removing in that session, stand quietly for a moment. Watch as the disc slowly moves away.

Then, visualize the sun beams above your head, sending beautiful healing rays down through the canopy of trees and into your energy field. Feel the warmth of healing light radiating throughout your body, filling all the empty spaces from where denseness was removed. Allow yourself to be immersed in that energy momentarily and give thanks.

AUTOMATIC WRITING

When I first started channeling, I would use a method called automatic writing, also known as psychography. That is when you channel information through your own stream of consciousness in the form of writing. Essentially, I would receive information through my thoughts and I would write them down. I would sit with the intention of receiving information from my guides for my highest good. After protecting myself, I would sit with a pen and paper. I would relax my mind through mindful breathing, and when I felt the urge to write, I would put my pen to paper, and I would begin writing. I wouldn't think about what I was writing; rather, I would allow the messages to come through as my own thoughts and I would write them down. I wouldn't read the messages at all until I was done. At that time, I was new to channeling, and I couldn't believe how easy it was to receive guidance that way.

From that point, I used automatic writing to communicate with my guides and my higher self. It was my primary method of communication and how I received most of my guidance from spirit. I had stacks of journals filled with channeled messages. For the first few years, I only tried to get information for myself and my family. It was a great tool to guide me through some major transitions in my life. Once I felt comfortable, I would receive guidance for my clients using this method. Eventually, I started teaching others how to do it themselves. I have taught a lot of esoteric-centered classes over the years, and this was the one that yielded the most results.

I wanted to include this method in the book because I feel like it is such a valuable tool for people to connect with their higher guidance on their own. I want to be clear that I am not encouraging anyone to channel entities using their body. There are a lot of definitions for channeling. One mainstream style is to invite an entity to come into your body and speak through you. Generally, when that occurs, there is an audience listening, and the messages are for a group of people. I do not recommend that anyone try this without proper training, and even with training, I don't believe this is safe to do. Another method of channeling is telepathic communication. When you connect with a guide or your higher self, the messages come through as your own thoughts. Sometimes, messages from guides or other beings can be perceived audibly, but the most common way is through telepathy.

Channeling through telepathy is, in my opinion, the safest way to receive messages. That's not to say that you can't be fooled by negative entities masking themselves as an angel or a spirit guide. Be sure to be diligent with your spiritual hygiene and clear in your intentions of who you are connecting with, and always use discernment when receiving messages. If something feels off, stop the session and ground and clear yourself. Try again another day when you feel you are at a higher vibration. That being said, if you feel good about your connection and it feels safe. People tend to read the message and analyze it too much. It's common to think you are making it up, but try to dismiss that as best you can. Trust your intuition, and, over time, you will have the potential to receive more information than you ever dreamed of.

The Process of Automatic Writing

Sit in a comfortable and quiet space, free of distraction. Use your favorite methods of protection and relaxation before you begin. When I started automatic writing, I would play 432hz music in the background to help me relax while connecting. You can play any music that makes you feel at peace; I recommend choosing something without words.

That way, you resist the urge to sing along to the song. Play something soothing and relaxing that will complement your session.

Initially, I recommend you resist the urge to connect to one of your guides and focus on connecting to your higher self. I can almost guarantee that you can receive anything you want to know by asking your soul. Remember that our souls are connected to the collective consciousness, where all information is stored. So, technically, we don't need to seek beyond ourselves to receive guidance since we are fully capable of connecting to the quantum information web. Of course, our guides and soul families are there to protect us and guide us as needed, but their biggest request is that the human species regain their abilities by activating them through methods such as this one. Once you get comfortable with channeling from your own soul, practice receiving messages from your star family, and have fun with it. Remember to use intention, and make sure you are clear that you only consent to connect to beings of the light, who are there for your highest good only!

Once you are ready, set the intention to connect to your higher self to receive guidance that is necessary at that time for you to hear that is in alignment with your highest good. Have your pen and paper ready. Close your eyes, relax, and wait until you begin to feel a stream of thought flow through. When that occurs, open your eyes and begin to write. Don't worry about handwriting, spelling, grammar, or anything else. Resist the urge to read your writing; don't stop until you feel you are done. Then, put the pen down and read without judgment or ridicule. The first time, you may write one word, one sentence, or a lot more. There is no right or wrong. This is a process that takes patience and practice. Some people are going to do this for the first time and be natural at it. Others may take a few times to get the flow going. Try not to compare yourself to anyone else and how much they can write. If you have any visions, write those down too.

Keep a journal; every time you do this exercise, write the date and keep a sequential order. That way you can go back and review. Sometimes, messages won't make sense at first, but when you look back at several messages, there may be a pattern or an *Ah-ha* moment. I can't recommend this method enough. I have taught this to children as young as ten with great success. I believe children are more open than adults, so they can often do these types of exercises much faster. I have also taught this to countless adults with great success.

Give it a try, and if you don't succeed at first, try again when you feel like the timing is right. I put this technique towards the end of this book section because I recommend trying other exercises to release blocks, negative cords, and limiting beliefs first. That way, when you try something like this, you are in a higher vibration and potentially ready for this step.

ANCESTRAL HEALING

In my previous book, I wrote about ancestral healing; however, I have learned more in the past year that I feel inclined to share. I have learned that almost everyone incarnated into this timeline is here to do some level of ancestral healing. I have been shown through my sessions that there are collectives here to do a higher level of purifying the ancestral lines, yet everyone is playing their role. I see a high volume of people utilizing their bodies as conduits of healing, which I feel is extremely important to share. For example, there is a large percentage of the population here to heal the divine feminine womb. Through thousands of years of suppression and enslavement, the collective womb has suffered massive amounts of abuse. I have a lot of clients that were female in a past life where they were raped, enslaved, or used within sex trafficking operations. The excessive nature of womb trauma will likely never be uncovered. Still, the important thing is that the process of healing has begun.

What I have uncovered in my sessions is the method by which the body transmutes collective trauma. Since we are all connected through energetic pathways, our cells can regenerate within the frequency of trauma, even in a different lifetime. If a person comes here to do ancestral healing of the womb, her cells will become triggered when it becomes time for the healing to begin. This can be a predetermined timeframe decided ahead of time in the life planning stage. It can occur during childhood, young adulthood, or even after menopause. There are many ways the body can clear the collective trauma, one of which is through menstruation. Heavy periods can indicate the purging of the collective trauma through the uterus. Endometriosis and other inflammatory conditions within the uterus can be caused by excess energy flowing through that region, which the sacral chakra activates. I have even had women who have needed total hysterectomies because their wombs could no longer purge the trauma. Instead, the uterus was removed, thereby releasing the trauma altogether. The amazing thing is that this process can heal thousands of other women connected to them from their ancestral line and/or soul family network.

There are a lot of Indigenous cultures working through genocide trauma healing. In this case, volunteers come into this timeline to heal the souls connected to the tribe that endured the trauma. The connection between a person healing the trauma and the souls receiving the trauma can have many layers. First, the souls receiving the healing don't have to be living; most of the souls have passed on. Secondly, they can be souls within their soul family who have been incarnated together for many cycles yet are not necessarily related in the human sense. Lastly, the connection can be purely based on genetics and the souls directly connected to the human family lineage.

Many people have appendectomies, nephrectomies, thyroidectomies, hepatectomies, lobectomies, and more. In many of these cases, the organ becomes full of toxic energy, and the body can't transmute it any longer, so a piece of the organ or the entire organ is removed. These people volunteered to use their bodies as conduits of healing to accelerate the collective healing process by taking a large percentage of the trauma energy through their bodies. Once the organ is removed, there is closure of the trauma loop. There is no way for one person to do this level of transmuting for the collective, so thousands of volunteers agreed to take this on. Most of the population in the ascension timeline has volunteered to assist in a lower level of physical integration so their health issues wouldn't be as severe. Nonetheless,

I didn't realize the level at which our collective ancestral healing is taking place, which will likely continue for many years.

If you are reading this thinking you could be one of those volunteers, take a deep sigh of relief. That means your health conditions have potentially been for the greater good of humanity. For those of my clients that I have received direct messages that they are, in fact, here to do some level of ancestral healing, I tell them all the same thing. This information can be very empowering because it can shift your outlook on your health. Once you stop resisting and place yourself in a seat of power, you can shift the tone. By recognizing that you agreed to use your body as a conduit in this life, you can shift your mindset to, *how can I help?* Instead, many people go to doctor after doctor, being prescribed medications with no root cause diagnosis. I have found ways to assist the body throughout this process to reduce resistance. I will share my favorite techniques with you later in the book, but for now, I want to share the mental aspect of the healing process.

When we are in fear, we tend to go into survival mode. I have shared some ways the body reacts during *fight-or-flight*, and one primary reaction is to accelerate the symptoms. If a post-menopausal woman has been to the doctor about the sudden onset of bleeding. Yet, all tests come back within normal limits. In that case, it's natural to become frustrated. This frustration can lower her vibration, which causes the body to work harder to transmute the trauma energy within her womb. This can trigger heavier bleeding, and then the body must compensate, which can cause frequent urination, sweating, and/or diarrhea. Why does this occur? When the body is transmuting energy, it must have a method to release it. The body can release through breath, tears, urination, defecation, sweating, and other bodily fluids.

The lymphatic system works tirelessly to ensure that nothing harmful spreads throughout the body. So, if the body can't release what it needs from one pathway, it will find another close by. The process is pretty ingenious. My point in all of this is that our body is transmuting a lot more than we realize, and the best way to support it is through thought and emotion. If you shift your thoughts and create an affirmation to support your body, the emotions connected to the condition can shift to excitement and joy to be a part of something so incredible. I am not saying that you should jump for joy when you have a health condition. Rather, if you suspect it is ancestral healing related, you can take charge by saying, *"I embrace the healing and transmuting that is occurring in my body, and I surrender to it. I no longer resist the process. I am grateful to be part of the collective healing. I am happy and willing to utilize my body as a conduit, so long as it is in alignment with my highest good."*

This simple shift in consciousness can change everything. Your body will move out of *fight-or-flight* and shift into healing mode. Your mindset will be much more empowered and supportive of the process. Even better, the process can occur much faster and less intense. I want to be clear that even if you do not suspect ancestral healing as the root cause of your illness, you can still shift your mindset to allow for optimal healing to occur where your mind and body work together. You can create a similar affirmation, such as, *"I embrace the healing and transmuting process occurring in my body, and I surrender to it. I no longer resist the process. I am grateful that I have already healed and am shifting into alignment with my highest good."*

CALLING ON THE ANIMAL KINGDOM

As many of you know, I have a deep connection and respect for the animal kingdom. In my previous book, I spoke about the many ways animals can guide us throughout our lives. I wanted to add to that information by sharing a powerful story and protection meditation in this book. I will start by sharing how I was prompted to call on the animal kingdom for protection. Many years ago, when I was thirsty for esoteric knowledge, I took a shamanic healing class with a local energy healer. A friend of mine had worked with her before and said she was a powerful healer and mentor. She offered an in-depth shamanic healing course that was split up into levels. Each level was an entire weekend. I even hosted one of the weekend workshops at my wellness center.

I was so excited to take this course because shamanic healing always intrigued me. In hindsight, I was probably so excited to work with this lady I was blind to all the red flags. She was a pretty woman, charming, outgoing, and extremely confident in her knowledge. When I took level one that first weekend, there weren't too many red flags other than her teaching style, which was a little arrogant for me. I don't like it when people act like they are better than the people they are teaching. As a teacher myself, I am always humbled at the thought of what my mentees are experts on and what I can learn from them. We all have something to contribute, so making people feel inferior because you happen to know about something other people are interested in is absurd. During the first weekend's class, I noticed that she was pushy about what she was teaching and wasn't open to anything contradicting what she believed to be true. Mind you, this class was not a bunch of amateurs. Many of the students were reiki masters and professional healers. So, the baseline knowledge of the collective group was quite extensive. Perhaps this made her uncomfortable because some of us had healing styles that didn't align with hers.

When we started level two, things started to get weird. People in the class became very emotional and unstable. The class vibe was off, and I noticed the red flags more and more. She shared an intimate story with us during one of the days about how she crossed paths with a demon many years prior when she was on holiday overseas. She shared how shaken she was by the experience because she claimed to lock eyes with the demon, and it was caught off guard when it realized she could see him. She told us how much that experience affected her, and she was never the same again. Thinking back, I wonder why she shared that story and why that wasn't enough for me to walk away. I guess I was intrigued by this lady's life, so I kept allowing her to teach me. Later, I realized that the experience she had with the dark entity opened the door for an attachment that she didn't know she had. I believe that demon attached to her the moment they locked eyes and remained with her until that present day. Who knows, maybe it is still with her.

I could share many other red flags, but I will skip to the end. As soon as I removed myself from the envy vibration, I reclaimed my power and saw her for who and what she was. She was pretending to teach shamanic methods to her mentees while she siphoned their power and drained their energy. I believe she intended to create a cult for herself and her demon to feed off, as well as the clients her graduates would work on in the future. Needless to say, when I dropped out of the course, she reacted. At first, she was very cordial and sent me countless emails, voice messages, and texts trying to get me back. When I say I cut her off, I cut her off. As soon as I let her know I wouldn't be continuing, I blocked her, deleted all emails and correspondence, and threw all her material in the trash, along with anything she ever gave me. That might sound harsh, but wait until I finish the story.

The abrupt severing of our energetic connection prompted her demon to come to attack me, which I was expecting. I could hear growling and snarling in my ears, scary laughter, screeching sounds, dark images, and many other things over the next few weeks. I did all the clearings and affirmations I knew how to do, and I had a trusted friend do an extensive clearing on me. This torture lasted for several weeks. She was incessant and wouldn't stop attacking me on a psychic level. We never saw each other or crossed paths after I left her program, so everything that was occurring was on an energetic level. One night, I lay in bed and heard dogs growling at me; I was afraid and didn't know what to do. I activated a crystal grid of protection around my house, and she just laughed at me like I was pitiful. In my amateur days, I didn't think about protecting underneath my house. I visualized a protective shield around my house, like a perimeter fence. At this point, she said to me in a horrid voice, *"You don't think I can enter from under your fence!"*

At that point, I was legitimately scared and didn't know what to do. She had gotten to me. In that moment of desperation, I heard an angelic voice in my head telling me to call upon the animal kingdom for protection. It's almost as if something clicked in my mind, and I knew what to do. I became confident and secure in my knowing. In my mind, I called the animal spirits of the light to come to my home and to protect me in all dimensions and all aspects of my property. Within seconds, I could hear the animals coming. I heard the sounds of tigers growling, wolves howling, elephants trumpeting, and birds squawking. I saw herds of animals beginning to surround my home. Spiders, lizards, monkeys, leopards, and snakes were in the trees. Under my home were worms, insects, groundhogs, and other burrowing animals. In the sky above my home were hawks, dragons, eagles, ravens, and falcons. Around my home were bears, tigers, wolves, elephants, horses, giraffes, hippos, and buffalo. In my home was a pride of lions fanning out into each room. All of this occurred within seconds, and just like that, she was gone. She never came back, and I was never bothered again!

I sat in bed crying tears of joy. I couldn't believe the power of the animal kingdom and how they saved me. From that day forward, I called on them nightly to protect myself and my family. I encourage everyone to try this at least once. You will be pleasantly surprised by how quickly the animal spirits will come and how happy they are to protect us. It's almost as if they were already there that night, just waiting for my command.

Calling on the Animal Kingdom

I recommend calling on the animals to protect you before sleep time. You can even assign an animal to protect you while you travel the astral realm. I do this for myself and my children. The process of calling the animal spirits to you is simple. Set the intention that you are calling on the animal kingdom to protect you in your home, car, hotel room, office, classroom, or wherever you are. You can call on them to protect your family and your pets. Close your eyes, and as you set the intention, visualize a variety of animals coming into your space. Visualize them in all dimensions and all corners of your space: in the sky, around the perimeter, within your space, and underground. Listen to their sounds. Feel the energy of your space shift.

Assign one animal you feel connected with to be in your space while you sleep. Request that they remain with you in the physical and the astral realms to ensure you are safe and protected. You can do the same for the members of your family. Visualize that animal in their rooms next to their beds. Ask them not to leave until they wake up and return from their astral travels. You can also ask the animal spirits to remain with you throughout the day or assign a different animal for daytime protection. There are no limits. What you request will be, so long as you believe it to be so. Never underestimate the power of the animal spirits. They are here as our guardians, our teachers, and our protectors. If you cherish your connection with them as a sacred union and you have gratitude for their assistance, there is no limit to what they can do to help us.

PART THREE

THE DAWN OF FREEDOM

In this section of the book, I want to share with you some powerful soul collectives I have encountered. Many of you reading this may resonate with one of these groups which may activate something within you. I have spoken about different groups over the years, such as Indigos, Crystals, Stars, Rainbows, Divine, The Artemis Collective, and many more. My intention for sharing this information so as not to box people into a group. We have seen enough of that within the 3D box. It is essential to share this information because so many people feel so different from their family and peers that it creates a sense of not belonging. I believe many Starseeds are purposely spread worldwide to impact more of the population. Because of this, there may not be many people like you in your community. When I share details from these soul groups, and they resonate with people, they begin to feel like they are not alone. Even though they may be the only ones in their town from a particular collective, they find comfort in knowing there are others like them somewhere.

THE HALO GROUP

I first learned about the Halo Group in 2021 during a session with a middle-aged female of Asian descent. She was born in Japan and moved to the United States as a teen exchange student. She never felt connected to her culture and struggled to find purpose throughout her life. When she was a teenager, she was deeply depressed and longed to leave her country to explore the world. In her session, I was told she is part of a group of divine feminine souls from Sirius A called the Halos. They get their name because they have a beautiful white and golden hue of light around them. This Halo of light is separate from their auric field. It's an expanded energetic band of light that keeps them disconnected from the third dimension so they don't become trapped within it. I was told that the Halo group is similar to Earth Angels because they are very calm, peaceful, and loving beings who come to the planet to assist humanity in the darkest places.

Since 2021, I have had countless more clients connected to the Halo group, which has given me the opportunity to gather more information on this soul collective. Exclusively talking about my clients and what I have learned from their sessions, it appears they are all from Sirius A or B. They work closely with Earth Angels because they have a similar energy of peace, and their frequency is almost identical to the angelic realm. The difference between the Halo group and angels is that they bring in knowledge of ascension from their own lineage of existence. They are ascended beings of light who come here to assist in the breakdown of masculine control, fear paradigms, suppression of women, and manipulation from the dark players.

The Halo group incarnates in three continents: Asia, Europe, and North America. There tends to be a heavy influence in China, Korea, Japan, Taiwan, Iran, Iraq, Syria, Turkey, Russia, Bulgaria, Serbia, Poland, the United States, and Canada. It seems like they don't all stay in their countries of birth, and there could be Halo souls all over the globe. The purpose of their being born into those countries is to slowly shift the genetics of their culture by bringing more light into their bodies, which, over time, will shift the future generations. They also positively impact the energetic blueprint of their region because they are doing grid work from the moment they are born.

Grid work is when the frequency of a person's light, or their soul signature, vibrates out of their body and into the environment. This can significantly impact the negative energy waves in the atmosphere as they slowly transmute to lower frequencies. They also emit a frequency of light that travels through their feet and into the ground beneath them, which shifts lay lines and works to re-grid the planetary energy positively. Their Halo is part of a frequency band of light that can instantly transmute negative energy. Generations of submission, power, and masculine control can be seen in the quantum field as a dense, dark energy hue. The Halo light can break this dense energy down slowly over time. However, there needs to be thousands of volunteers to make a lasting impact.

A majority of Halo souls tend to choose a neglectful and abusive family. They don't receive a lot of love and support growing up. They tend to feel like they are in the wrong culture, or at the very least, they strongly disagree with their culture's philosophies. They feel lonely throughout their life, and some choose to experience abusive relationships. I've noticed that many of the Halo group are working on their voice in this life and tend to have a blocked throat chakra. I have seen a lot of masculine dominance within this group, so working through self-confidence, self-love, and acceptance is a crucial theme.

The blueprint for this group seems to be a personal journey of strength and endurance. Once they are able to achieve a certain level of self-love through profound healing and discovering their power, they can find the strength to stand proud in their divine feminine energy.

Another theme for this group, as for many others, is ancestral healing. There are thousands of souls within their ancestral and soul lineage that have endured masculine control, enslavement, and soul fragmenting over many thousands of years. The Halo group has chosen to incarnate in areas of the world with masculine control, feminine suppression, fear tactics, authoritative leadership, power struggles, hierarchy of rights, and emotionally reserved citizens. As the Halo group incarnates within these cultures to experience similar traumas, they slowly heal their soul, which also transmutes the trauma for their ancestral and soul lineage. They can slowly shift the culture by inserting their frequencies of love, empathy, compassion, openness, inclusiveness, and creativity. Over time, a new generation will be born.

I had another session with a woman in the Halo group, and she received a message from one of her guides, an elder within the Halo collective. I have shared a portion of it below.

"My dear sister of light, you are among a very special group of light beings on Earth from Sirius. You can compare our energy and light to that of angels on Earth. We are pure light with a halo around our physical bodies to protect us in the Earth's atmosphere. Most of us choose to incarnate into an area of the world that is in deep need of assistance. Asian, Middle Eastern and Russian countries are among the most heavily influenced cultures, from power, wars, greed, manipulation, and control. Asian cultures were infiltrated thousands of years ago by powerful extraterrestrial beings who observed that their culture was highly susceptible to influence due to their docile nature. They have been programmed throughout generations to be submissive and follow orders. Women lost their rights and were bred

to be submissive to men, and their role was to care for the men and children. They lost their voice and, therefore, their essence. This is the same for Russian culture and in the Middle East. Volunteers from Halo of Light (a group made up of only women of Sirius A and B) came to Earth to regain the balance of feminine and masculine energy. After many thousands of years, we are able to see the impact of, not only our group on Earth, but the millions of other light beings that have volunteered to come from other collectives. We have worked closely with the Arcturians and the Pleiadians to anchor light in all areas of the planet to combat the dark. You are a truly special soul with a halo signature around you to remind you of who you are."

In 2023, I learned about a newer wave of Halo's that are in their teens and twenties. So far, all of them have been the daughters of a Halo Spirit, here to carry on the Halo work. This group came in with a slightly different energy band. Their Halo of light looks more like a golden sun aura. Their role is to bring new life and new energetic pathways to the planet. They are interested in childbirth, coaching, teaching, healing, and being of service to humanity. They all seem to have a very humble nature and are extremely loving and compassionate souls.

As I continue to meet new clients within the Halo Collective, I am sure there is a lot more to discover. Perhaps there is another wave being born at this very moment that will play a role in future discoveries, healing, and leadership. Only time will tell.

THE SUN RAYS

I learned about the Sun Ray Collective in 2023. Several of my clients are within this group of ascended beings that are fractals of light from the consciousness of the Sun. I learned that the Sun is a conscious ball of light that is activated, continuously expanding, and contracting as new souls come in and out of this galaxy. The light that makes up the Sun is part of God, a fractal of Source creation, and within it is the life force energy of the universe. Just like each and every soul is a fractal of God, the Sun is many fractals of God combined together to create the heartbeat of each galaxy.

The Sun Rays are fractals of the consciousness of the Sun that are mostly pure light. They volunteer to incarnate on this planet to break down the 3D attempt to block out the Sun. When they embody a human form, they are able to anchor to the planetary grid. All human beings do this because our bodies are made of Earth matter; therefore, we are part of the Earth. Their spiritual DNA has sunlight codes embedded within it, and those light codes vibrate out to the environment throughout their life. The Sun Rays literally spread the Sun DNA all over the planet. Sun Rays can be of all ages and live in all areas of the world. They tend to be very gentle people who love nature, animals, and water. Many Sun Rays live near the ocean and care deeply about marine life. I have seen several Sun Rays going into the field of conservation and marine biology.

What do we Need to Know About the Sun?

During my sessions with my clients who are part of this collective, I have been shown significant benefits of the Sun and misconceptions spread by the dark players. I will do my best to review what I have learned in the following few pages.

The Sun breathes light codes, cosmic data, and solar energy. When it exhales, it sends waves of energy to the other planets within our galaxy. There are many suns within infinite galaxies spread throughout the multi-verse.

The Sun is a portal. To expand on that, I have been shown that the Sun has many portals that serve as pathways for souls to travel in and out of this galaxy. There are souls that have the essence of the Sun's consciousness and are guardians of the portals and the light codes being released. I have learned that many thousands of sun souls have formed a collective called the Sun Rays that started incarnating on the planet about 100 years ago to assist in the breakdown of the third-dimensional firmament that was created to block out the Sun's rays.

Our ancestors worshiped Sun Gods such as Helios, Ra, and Sol. Regardless of which deity was worshipped, their people believed these souls were representations of the Sun. Therefore, they held within them the power and strength of the Sun. They believed the Sun bestowed the light and wisdom of the cosmos. They knew the strength of the Sun's rays and how they would not only heal the body, but fill the body with light codes, knowledge, and nourishment.

The dark players know the powers of the Sun which is why they have made countless attempts over generations to block the Sun's rays and invert the truth about the Sun. From what I am told, climate change agendas began as an attempt to spread false information about the condition of our planet's longevity to insert more layers of deceit. Climate change was the focal point for the dark players to begin weather warfare through extreme temperature shifts, unprecedented storms, floods, and earthquakes. This led to hybridized agriculture, bioengineered food, and lab-grown meat, all in the name of climate change.

In the late '80s and '90s, a fear campaign headlining the negative effects of the Sun began to travel through humanity like a virus. I can recall an increase in the use of sunblock and sunglasses in the early 2000s. In current sessions, I have been informed that the dark players' attempts to scare people from the Sun's *harmful effects* caused a massive shift in humanity, resulting in people spending much more time indoors than in previous generations. The dark players led people to believe that the Sun was more harmful than beneficial to our health. As a result, excessive sunblock use, UV-protectant clothing, hats, and sunglasses have been inserted into our normal everyday lives.

Instead of receiving healing, light codes, nourishment, and vitamin D from the Sun's rays, humanity has been sheltering indoors under artificial lighting and swallowing capsules to receive their dose of vitamin D. Trees, plants, flowers, and fruit receive most of their nourishment from the Sun, and in my opinion, it would be a logical assessment that humans would similarly thrive with the benefit of the Sun. The planet receives the same Sun's rays embedded with cosmic information, light codes, and nutritional benefits as humans do. There are Moon cycles that cleanse and purify the planet. At the same time, the Sun breathes new life and energy into the atmosphere for all living beings to absorb.

One example of this is during an eclipse. The Sun continuously sends the planets within its galaxy waves and waves of activating energy and abundant light. The Sun expands and contracts energetically with every moment. During an eclipse, the Moon overlaps the Sun precisely for a few minutes. The process can take hours, but the moment of the eclipse doesn't last long. I have been shown in several sessions that during this pause of energy transformation, the Sun builds up a charge of necessary energetic codes, which amplify as the Sun essentially holds its breath for a moment. Once the Moon shifts away from the Sun, the Sun exhales by releasing massive waves of energy toward the planets and souls that are ready to receive it.

The Sun has powerful sequences of quantum and interstellar data emitted through portals and the Sun's rays. The human eyes receive this data, uploaded through the pineal gland, where consciousness activations occur. When a person wears sunglasses, their eyes cannot receive the data because the lens blocks it. This prevents the person from receiving and processing the activation sequences and information being sent from the universe. By blocking the eyes from the sun, the body cannot adequately protect the skin from too much sun exposure, which can cause skin burning.

When the eyes perceive sunlight, the body produces melanin, a pigment that causes your skin to darken and protects it from the Sun's UV rays. If sunlight is blocked due to sunglasses, the body doesn't receive the signal to produce melanin. The cool thing is that the skin also has sun receptors telling the body to increase melanin production. However, if a person is wearing sunglasses and has sunblock slathered all over their skin, the melanin production will be limited. Sunblock is filled with toxic chemicals that act as a barrier to the skin. If a film of toxic lotion blocks the skin, it won't be able to perceive the Sun's rays; furthermore, it won't be able to breathe. The skin breathes by opening the pores that are all over the body. There are thousands of pores on our skin, and as we sweat, we release toxins and energetic waste. I believe that preventing the skin from breathing out toxins and putting more toxins on the skin, such as sunblock, make-up, toxic clothes, perfumes, and dyes, is why skin cancer is so high.

Another anomaly of being in the sun is that people feel tired, even drained, after being in the sun for prolonged periods. During my sessions, I learned a lot of interesting facts. While a living being is in direct sunlight, their body receives healing, upgrades, and light codes. This applies to humans, animals, rocks, plants, water, and trees. The Sun can assist a human on a physiological level as well as on a soul level. The conscious mind can't interpret much of the information received; however, the soul receives information that the higher self-interprets. This can be hard on the physical body as it gets all the new data and needs processing time. This can cause a person to be sleepy and drained after spending even small amounts of time in the sun. Sleep helps the body process and heal.

The unfortunate part about the dark players' misinformation agenda on the magical powers of the Sun is that there is an abundance of disinformation available. If anyone does an internet search on the benefits of the Sun, harmful effects of sunblock, sunglasses, melanin, sweating toxins, or anything similar, there are endless sites spreading fear and misguidance. One thing I have learned in my spiritual journey is that if the dark players try too hard to convince us of anything, it's likely false information.

I encourage those of you reading this to use discernment and decide for yourself what you believe and what you are willing to explore further. There are simple ways to develop a healthy relationship with the Sun. I recommend you take your time with sun exposure, especially if you have been avoiding the sun out of fear. Take gradual steps so that your body can acclimate to the Sun's frequency. Sungazing is a powerful method of receiving Sun codes without looking directly at harsh light. During sunrise and sunset, the Sun's rays are not as powerful and are softer on the eyes. You can start with a few moments of sungazing and work your way up over time. Even small doses of sunlight in your eyes can have lasting effects.

During daylight hours, try taking your sunglasses off for brief periods to allow your eyes to get used to the brightness of the Sun. I believe it is ok to wear sunglasses if you devote time throughout the day for natural light to travel through your eyes directly with no filter. You don't have to stare directly at the Sun. I don't recommend this unless you are very comfortable with the sunlight and this is something you have practiced.

Heliotherapy is another way to absorb the sun in small doses. By sitting in the sun for small increments, such as ten to fifteen minutes, the skin can breathe the Sun's rays into the body and receive light codes that can enhance the immune system, balance the body, and promote overall well-being. The more your body is used to heliotherapy, the longer you can sit in the sun without burning. You must take your time and go with the flow of your body. When I do heliotherapy, I sit for forty-five minutes to one hour. I can sit that long without burning because I have been in the sun my whole life and am very used to the Sun's rays.

It is evident that the animal kingdom is aware of heliotherapy, and they take advantage of it regularly. My dogs will go outside in the yard and sit directly in the sun for short periods, and they move to the shade when they have had enough. It's as if their body has an innate knowledge of how much sun therapy they need. My hairless cat spends most of the day on our screened-in patio. There is plenty of shade and areas with a lot of sun. I watch him move throughout the day in and out of the sun, and I can only assume he is acutely aware when he has had enough sun, and he knows to move into the shade.

We can also see this in the animal kingdom. We have a drive-through animal safari park near our house in Florida and have gone dozens of times. In the middle of summer, when it is full sun and very hot out, almost all the animals are under the pavilions, dens, or huddled under the tree branches. We have also seen them basking in the sun, seemingly content with the sun exposure. I believe animals seek out the sun when they need vital nourishment and know when to retreat to cool their bodies down.

Positive Benefits of the Sun

- Increases dopamine and serotonin.

- Opens the pineal gland.

- Stimulates melanin, which can reduce skin cancer.

- Stimulates mitochondrial production and prolonged energy.

- Promotes a healthy immune system.

- Reduces anxiety.

- Improves sleep cycles and circadian signaling.

THE SUPERNOVAS

I have known about a collective called the Supernovas for many years. I never thought much about them until I started attracting clients within this group in 2023 and 2024. The most profound session I had was with a girl in her late teens, living in the U.S. She was a lovely girl finishing her senior year of high school and was interested in studying marine biology in college. When I first connected to her soul, I was shown a Mer-person living during the time of Lemuria. I was told she was part of a soul collective called the Supernovas and was not from this universe. I was told that Supernovas assist in eras of collapse on different planets to assist in the birth of a new era, and they only incarnate within civilizations that choose ascension. Otherwise, planets that are being destroyed by their inhabitants will self-destruct in an attempt to reboot and heal.

They explained that the human collective living within 3D on Earth had chosen the ascension path. So, a new wave of energy and light was being sent to the planet to assist in the transcendence of the souls within the matrix. In essence, a new birth occurs while the darkness is pulled within a black hole. From there, souls are placed within a lower density to create or join a similar 3D reality. I was told they would travel to another realm where they could continue in a low vibration of their resonance, and the most fractured and lost souls would return to Source to be re-joined with the consciousness of One.

I was told that there are thousands of Supernovas spread all over the planet, and they can be of any age. The older generations of Supernovas came in to lay the groundwork for the future generations that would come in at the tail end of the ascension period. I believe that the older generation of Supernovas has struggled more than almost any soul collective group. This is because they have felt like *fish out of water* during the densest, most challenging times in 3D history. It is my innerstanding that throughout history, when previous ascension periods surfaced, Supernovas incarnated in smaller numbers than today. Because there weren't enough lightworkers on the planet to awaken humanity, those ascensions never came to fruition. That is why this era is so significant, because, I am told, this is the farthest humanity has come to break out of 3D.

A new wave of Supernovas started coming into a timeline of great significance because this is the era of change. I was told they started coming in during the mid-1950s, and there are thousands of them here, holding the space for transition and evolution. Many in this group have struggled greatly because they have known they are different their whole life. They tend to find comfort and solace near water; therefore, many of them choose to live near the ocean. Like the Sun Rays, they tend to have an interest in marine biology, animals, and conservation. They are extremely sensitive and don't do well with conflict.

As I mentioned, the Supernova collective doesn't incarnate into planets that have not reached a trajectory of ascension. Their souls are very pure and they don't wish to descend to lower densities unless an evolutionary path is secured. Through my sessions with several adult women, I was told they would bring in the next wave of Supernovas. As far as I know, there aren't any from this wave born yet. They are holding the space energetically and supporting their parents' journey so they can prepare for their arrival. I haven't received a timeframe of when they will begin incarnating; however, I have been told it will be within the next one to two years. There are a few reasons they are waiting. First, the collective awakening hasn't yet reached the percentage they are waiting for. I have been told in different sessions that the percentage of awakened souls within the 3D was approaching 40% as of 2022. I have even heard we have reached over 50% as of 2024. I have not been told what the exact percentage of people needed to be awake in order for the next wave of Supernovas to come through. In my opinion, it has more to do with the breakdown of the 3D. It's not so much about the number of people; instead, it's about the over-all frequency.

The more people elevate their frequency and hold the space for transition, the more the matrix will be broken down. As the matrix breaks down, more light comes through, as well as beings of even higher densities of consciousness. There are so many variables that are not limited to time, space, or a dimension. The great awakening is a multidimensional paradigm of ever-changing energy and trajectories based on the collective frequencies of souls within the 3D. Collectively, we can influence the timing, the speed, and the overall outcome by holding the space of sovereignty. The next wave of Supernovas is powerful, incorruptible, and beyond anything we have seen in many centuries. They will begin their physical journey to Earth from parallel universes once humanity has risen out of 3D and anchored into the fifth dimension.

The last thing I want to say about Supernovas is that they bring me great comfort and excitement. I have always gauged my validation of the ascension timeline on the new Earth children. I know they wouldn't come onto the planet if we weren't ready for change. Humanity must be at a point where we are prepared to help ourselves. When enough people have exited the mind control cycles, many advanced galactic and interdimensional beings will come to guide us. There are no saviors; there are guardians, mentors, and ascended beings of light that come to be a part of our evolution. They are not here to do the work for us. Supernovas bring so much wisdom because they have been a part of countless transition periods of planets like ours in even lower densities. They are compassionate, resilient, and have an innerstanding of our struggles. They see beyond all illusions projected by the box matrix; therefore, they can assist us in many ways.

LIVING IN THE NEUTRAL ZONE

*"Out beyond ideas of wrongdoing and rightdoing, there is a field,
I'll meet you there."*

-Rumi

The best advice I can give is to live within the neutral zone. There is no question that the collective anxiety over the past five years has risen exponentially. Because humanity is going through the 4th dimension, there are a lot of trigger points that are catalysts for emotional releases that transpire in many different ways. There are a lot of false saviors and controlled opposition implanted within the spiritually awakened community. The dark players' attempt to block the awakening has no limitation. Whether they use spiritual warfare, fear, agendas, celebrities, politicians, indoctrination, wars, chemtrails, weather warfare, or media manipulation of current events, they have not slowed down.

The dark players will create chaos, misinformation, and distraction to keep people plugged in and subscribed to the matrix because, if they have your attention, they can attempt to hold you hostage. The culture of division seems to be the most significant agenda within their playbook. As long as they can create sides, people will continue to point fingers at each other instead of looking at themselves and truly healing. They will trigger us with fear, anxiety, sadness, anger, rage, and judgement so that people remain in survival mode. The longer people are in survival mode, the harder it is to prioritize their wellness.

The resistance to healing is stronger when someone is in a frequency of desperation. They can't even imagine themselves in a better place or at peace when they don't know how they are going to give their children their next meal or continue to have a roof over their heads.

We certainly can't control the dark narrative. The bullies are going to kick us when we are down and create more and more drama for us to get sucked into. I always tell my children they can't control what other people will do, but they *can* control their reaction. Our reaction is our free will. We have the power to shift the energy that we give out through our thoughts and actions. As a result, we begin to control the narrative.

There are easy ways to slowly shift from being the back-seat driver of our lives in a reactionary position to the creator of our reality, in complete control of the driver's seat. We can do this by placing ourselves in a space of neutrality. During moments of division, when you want to choose a side or have a strong reaction to a situation, take a pause. Imagine yourself lifting out of the experience altogether and connecting with your higher self, the silent observer. Allow yourself to connect to the vibration of balance, void of emotion. Next, re-connect with the experience from the lens of that neutral perspective. Notice how your reaction shifts. Notice how your view of the other person or people shifts. Notice the different sides of the story, right, wrong, or indifferent to your perspective. By not having an emotionally charged reaction to the most challenging situations, you will find yourself more composed and balanced. You will be able to think clearly, and you will be less likely to fall into the traps of 3D programming and entity influence.

Every story has multiple sides: the people living the experience and the neutral perspective that sees all sides. One of my biggest lessons was when I learned that there are no ultimate truths. Everyone is right and wrong, all at the same time. That is why God allows souls to have authentic experiences so that they can learn from their perceptions.

Have you ever argued with someone where you couldn't figure out for the life of you why the other person couldn't innerstand where you were coming from? You were so sure of your truth that anything other than that was absurd, even insulting.

Meanwhile, they were living their end of the experience, likely feeling the same way. In hindsight, after time passed and you calmed down, I wonder if you felt as strongly as you did in the original moment. Many of us reflect upon our actions and wonder if we overreacted or judged too harshly. Needless to say, no one was wrong at that moment because each person was viewing and experiencing through their own lens of perception.

During heightened periods of the dark players' tactics and your life challenges, I recommend taking a step back and positioning yourself as the neutral observer, if only to see if your thoughts, conclusions, or emotional reactions change. Don't allow yourself to get sucked into drama. Don't get manipulated into choosing sides. Stand firm in your own power and practice the art of neutrality. I can assure you it will open your eyes to an entirely new world of multidimensional reality.

IT'S ALL ABOUT BALANCE

So many aspects of 3D are misaligned with the highest good of humanity. I have given a myriad of examples throughout this book and my previous book, *Starseeds and the Great Awakening*, to showcase our species' disbalance. This paradigm has been constructed to support a heavy left-brained mentality that has dominated the right brain to the extent of atrophy. Many people have lost touch with their creative and intuitive gifts, which has caused them to lack a vital aspect of their potential. As I see it, we need to incorporate a way to include the significance of the right hemisphere of thinking in order to rebuild the part of us that has been dormant. I also recognize there are a lot of Starseeds that are completely tapped into the right brain and are incredibly creative, imaginative, and intuitive. Many artists are this way, whether they are: musicians, painters, poets, or highly esoteric.

In my humble opinion, there needs to be a balance of both. However, I feel it is difficult for the majority to be equally balanced. There will always be a slight dominance on one side over the other for many factors related to our DNA, genetics, environmental exposure, preferences, and necessity. This is perfectly fine because the goal is to be as close to a homeostatic balance as possible while still honoring the person's authenticity.

I have a pretty good balance of both left and right brain tendencies. Still, I operate at my greatest potential when I am more grounded in the intuitive and creative side. Many people are going to operate at their greatest potential when they are slightly connected to the part of them that serves them the most. This means that there are a lot of people who thrive in the logical mindset. To extend this thought one step further, I believe we have the potential to be dominant in one aspect versus the other when it serves us best. Therefore, during specific periods, we may be more logical. We may be more creative in others, depending on what suits us. I believe that is the sweet spot.

Another aspect of the 3D paradigm is the disbalance of divine feminine and masculine energy. Throughout history, humanity has gone from a matriarchal to a patriarchal society. Even further, the dark players have worked tirelessly to dissolve the divine feminine. This has suited the dark players because it is well-known that divine feminine energy is sacred. Women are creators, master alchemists, manifestors, and great leaders. I believe women are innately very intuitive and difficult to manipulate. Therefore, the dark players inserted the movement to enslave and suppress women to slowly fragment the collective essence of the divine feminine over time. To some degree, the dark players have succeeded in creating a society that is masculine-driven, and women have become second best. Essentially, the third-dimensional matrix is a man's world.

Regardless of gender, we require a balance of both masculine and feminine energies to truly thrive. Historically, the dark players have cultivated a reality where men have been highly masculine and thus lack feminine energy. They were the providers, not the nurturers. Women were the nurturers, the mothers, and the caregivers who connected predominantly to their feminine side. I believe a movement occurred in the 1990s to early 2000s where the dark players reshuffled their agenda deck and inverted the paradigm. Through feminine movements and a high concentration of gay characters in movies, they were able to push a reversal of the masculine and feminine energies. These agendas pushed homosexuality, enticing men to tap into their feminine side. Men began wearing make-up, dressing in women's clothing, and speaking in a more feminine tone. Men, in general, regardless of sexual preference, have been modified due to large amounts of hormones in the food supply. In many areas of the world, the body structure of men has drastically changed. This alternative extreme has caused newer generations of men to have less physical endurance and more feminine qualities.

For women, the opposite occurred. Through extreme feminist movements, women became more dominant with the theme that *women can do anything men can do*. There are a lot of ways we can unpack that statement. At the root of its meaning, there are layers of truth. Yes, in many cases, women can do what men do. The question is, *should they*? There are no right or wrong answers to this; instead, there are variations of perspectives. Some may say women can do anything a man can, even better. Others might say women can do many things men can do, but there are limitations, such as physical strength and endurance due to primal human DNA. There is a reason that men were hunters and women were the gatherers many cycles ago. So, there is an element of truth to that. Lastly, others can say there are many things women can do that men can do, but a mild structure of roles is beneficial. This means women can do what they are best at while men can do what they are best at, and we can optimize output. The issue with that statement is the dark players have messed with the human psyche for so long that the human body doesn't even hold the same frequency codes anymore, so things have changed. Not all men are the same, and not all women are the same anymore.

Here lies the dilemma: *where do we go from here*? If you are asking my opinion, it's all about balance. Other than watching what you eat and where you get your food from, there isn't a lot we can do about hormone additives in the food, the water supply, and anywhere else they sneak them in. Aside from that, I believe everyone, regardless of their gender, should take a moment to reflect on their feminine and masculine meter. Women will naturally have more of a feminine side, yet exploring and allowing the masculine side to shine through is extremely important. Think about the analogy of a toolbox. Inside a toolbox is an assortment of things, depending on your needs. Each tool serves a purpose and does something different, yet they all complement each other. We have both masculine and feminine energy at our disposal within our toolbox. They both serve a purpose, and I believe it is our innate ability to tap into both.

For example, if a woman is a single mother, she has the burden of the caregiver and the nurturer. If she must work several jobs to support her family and pay the bills, she may be more present in her masculine energy to ensure they have what they need to survive. Conversely, if a man was raised by a single mother and grew up with sisters, he would likely have a dominant feminine side. Humans have an incredible ability to adapt to their environment, which, in the long term, can alter their personalities and even how they look at the world. I believe we all have the capability to tap into both aspects of ourselves; we are just not taught how to do so.

When society loses balance, people are more likely to lose touch with their north star, that part of themselves that knows what is best for them and what isn't. With consistent brainwashing that penetrates the collective, there is no end to the manipulation. This puts people in an uneasy state where they feel unsure of who they are. So many people are concerned about what everyone else is doing, what's popular, and what people think of them that they lose themselves in the shuffle. When this occurs, an opening is created for programming. The dis-balance in this world leads to dis-ease, which leads to confusion and desperation, and ultimately, society is ushered into whatever mold the dark players want. Like sheep being herded by a pack of dogs, society, at large, is being herded into a genderless, promiscuous, hive-minded, satanic, transhumanistic, dystopian era. The simplest foundational constructs facilitate this, and dis-balance is one of the main tools in *their* toolbox.

A GIRL NAMED STEPHANIE

When I was 23, I worked in a small veterinary practice. I was pregnant with my oldest son, Jordan. I became friends with a receptionist named Stephanie, who was a few years older than me. She had two children under three years old. She was not like anyone I had met before. She was kind and generous, and she had such a radiating energy. During this time in my life, I was still guarded, and I was working through a lot of anger. I felt myself on the verge of a profound shift, even if I didn't fully understand it. I think this had a lot to do with being pregnant because things in my life started to shift, and I began noticing things I never noticed before. There was something about Stephanie that made me feel safe. Even if we were similar in age, she affected me in ways I didn't fully understand until much later.

I went to work one day, but Stephanie did not show up for her shift. It was unlike her not to show up for a shift, and I remember having a bad feeling about it. I remember thinking it was probably child-related, and it was likely that one of her children was sick. Even so, it was not like her not to call. Several hours passed until we received a call. I will never forget the moment when the practice owner called us into the treatment area. He told us that Stephanie had an aneurysm that morning and died on the way to the hospital. I still get emotional writing about this day, which occurred over 20 years ago. Immediately, I thought about her children. I was devastated that someone so incredible could die so suddenly at such a young age with two innocent children left behind. This was early in my spiritual awakening, so I didn't understand soul contracts and soul journeys. I

~ 221 ~

just felt angry and resentful that someone so kind could vanish just like that.

What I didn't realize was that going to her funeral was going to change the trajectory of my life. I still remember her funeral like it happened yesterday. It was held at her church, which was so big it could hold hundreds of people. I walked into the funeral, and I saw her open casket at the front of the room, which seemed like a football field away from where I was standing. There was a long line of people waiting to say their goodbyes. I looked around the room, and every seat was taken. There were so many people there that they had a side room open with another 50 seats, which was almost full. A TV monitor was on the wall so people could watch the funeral service from the side room. I sat in that room, not knowing anyone. I remember thinking about how many people were at Stephanie's funeral. I thought to myself, she must have touched a lot of people's lives to have this kind of turnout. She profoundly affected me, and clearly, other people felt the same. It started me down a cascade of thoughts, like, if I were to die, who would come to my funeral? Who would care? I didn't even know a fraction of the people who attended Stephanie's funeral. I didn't have many friends then, which made me stop and think.

While the minister was reading excerpts of the Bible, I began to tune him out. I felt myself experiencing a profound awakening. It was like my body was there, but my consciousness was not. I don't fully recall everything that happened in those 20 minutes while the minister talked, but it was profound. I instantly knew I would work to be a better version of myself, to impact people's lives as Stephanie did for me. I was no longer going to walk in bitterness and resentment towards my past bullies and those who hurt me or stole my power. I was ready to walk a new path. I thought to myself at that funeral, one day, when I die, I will have a funeral with this many people, too, because my life is going to matter.

In hindsight, after having three children, many spiritual awakenings, and more life experience, I have realized something. I did walk a new path after that day, and I truly changed, a little at a time. I became more patient and open with a completely different outlook on life. After the birth of my first son, I was ready to be a better version of myself. I believe that Stephanie's imprint on me was part of why I was prepared for that. I have continued to improve throughout the years, and that process will never stop because we are constantly evolving. My grand epiphany, as I reflect on that day at Stephanie's funeral, is that it wasn't about *my* future funeral and how many people would show up. That was my immature conscious mind trying to make sense of a profound experience through the perspective of a young girl. In my mind, I thought the lesson was that throughout my life, if I could impact as many people as Stephanie did, one day, when I died, a lot of people would mourn my loss, too. It's as if the number of people who attended my future funeral would somehow determine how successful my life was.

I have learned throughout my journey that I am here to do my very best and to be of service to humanity in ways that I am capable of. The value of my life's contribution is not calculated by the number of people who care when I'm gone. Rather, it's about the impact I make while alive. All the lives I touch. All the families I guide. All the children I mentor. All the walls I break down. All the new pathways I create. That's what it's all about. It's a collection of milestones and victories that positively influence the growth of the collective consciousness. When you combine the victories and milestones of all the people on the planet, that is where the magic is. That is when things truly change. That is the freedom movement.

NOT ALL STARSEEDS ARE SPIRITUAL

Throughout my sessions, I have learned something fundamental. Not all Starseeds incarnate to have a spiritual experience. Many people are here to make an imprint on the souls attached to bodies anchored in 3D. Millions of souls have been trapped within the third-density consciousness for thousands of years. Generations of predictive programming, false illusions, and fear have imprisoned humans in a left-brain, analytical, and logical mindset. The foundation of the dark players' reality is built upon trickery that targets the primal part of the brain. Many areas of the world indoctrinate children throughout their primary and secondary years of education. This is achieved in many ways, such as standardized testing, a uniform curriculum, memorization, and a letter grade system. Children have little to no creative input in their education, and much like a factory, children pass through each grade memorizing and regurgitating information.

As the youth of today pass through indoctrination schools, they are ushered into colleges to choose a career path. A majority of good paying and stable careers are within corporations, finance, law, medical, administrative, government, licensing, scientists, and highly left-brained focused. The right-brain jobs are much harder to pursue because there is less stability, and they are not as respected. Artists, poets, musicians, healers, and those who desire to live through passion have the most challenging time making a living. Because of this, Starseeds needed to find another way to interact with people plugged into the mainstream workforce. That's when many highly intelligent

Starseeds came through from places like Andromeda, Alpha Centauri, Sirius, and other planets with advanced technology.

I believe there are a lot of adults within the mainstream workforce who are Starseeds disguised as *"regular 3D people"*. Many aren't spiritual or religious at all. They focus more on science, information, statistics, research, and new discoveries. They are different than most others in their field because they are still disconnected from the mainstream and don't subscribe to the *norms of 3D*. They are not into sports, politics, parties, and drama. They are generally called conspiracy theorists because they are researching UFOs, space, time-travel, parallel realities, galactic beings, Earth phenomena, past lives, ancient civilizations, sasquatch, and paranormal activity. They believe in a higher power and the cosmic connection of all life; however, they are not the type to dive deep into spiritual practices. It's not because they don't believe in the metaphysical; it's quite the contrary. They will not focus their time on those aspects of consciousness because, on a higher level, they know they are here for another reason. They need to be the children, the spouses, the co-workers, the bosses, the mentors, and the friends of the people who need their influence without a spiritual focus.

The division is another tactic used by the dark players. Whether through religion, gender, woke agendas, ethnicity, social status, sports, politics, or belief systems, they create division. The more humanity is divided, the more tension and animosity are made among the collective. This creates a low vibration, and when they add wars, mass conflict, drugs, alcohol, dark entities, and shadow beings, it amplifies the darkness like a *Gotham City*. Only the dark players want the entire world to operate like the fictitious *Gotham,* as portrayed by DC Comics, to energize and fuel the 3D box while the elite 1% benefit from it all.

There are a lot of Starseeds mixed in with different aspects of the collective with the intention of positively infiltrating from the inside. There are Starseeds that are within religious communities, the medical industry, law enforcement, politics, and heavily involved in government programs. To blend in, they become chameleons in their environment. This aims to affect the people they come in contact with on a soul level, energetically, and to plant seeds of thought within their consciousness. They do not need to teach them about crystals, past lives, angels, or anything outside their comfort zone. Rescue missions are not about healing the person but about getting the person out alive. This category of Starseeds is present within the collective to shift people out of their programming by engaging their intelligence and minds. If they can shift a person out of their loop, perhaps it will create new thought patterns that can lead them to profound awakenings. Once they begin to wake up, it is up to them to navigate their journey to heal the soul.

Never underestimate the power of planting a seed in someone's mind and then letting it go. Over time, the person will have other experiences and synchronicities. Like a trail of breadcrumbs, they will have the potential to make their way back to their own light. I believe this group of Starseeds is present in the collective awakening period to create a ripple effect among the *sheeple* and for those who are lost. They might come off as different, awkward, and anti-social, and some might be labeled with high-functioning autism, previously known as Asperger's. However, don't underestimate their wisdom and potential to be the scientists, architects, way-showers, explorers, inventors, and leaders of a new era.

WHAT'S YOUR ROLE?

"Be the change you wish to see in the world."

- Gandhi

Throughout the last few years, I have found myself asking what my role is in many aspects of my life. For example, *what is my role in the ascension? What is my role in my children's lives?* These might sound like basic questions. You might even respond, "W*ell, Sherri, you are your children's mother, and that is your role."* I would agree, but moving beyond the basic responsibility of being a mother, I would like to think about how I can support my children's sovereign journey as a human, separate from playing the role of their mom. I like to create an intention to allow my children to be their authentic selves without me influencing them to be something I want them to be. I recognize their soul has a mission here in this life, and I like to think about ways to support them.

The biggest challenge of being a parent is letting go of control. We want so desperately to protect our children that sometimes we forget they signed on for specific lessons and challenges, and sometimes we must step aside. We can do our best to guide them and give them unconditional love and support, but ultimately, we must allow them to fly. As parents, we can provide a safety net, teach them boundaries, and do our best to teach them how to ground and protect themselves, so if they fall, they get right back up and try again.

I encourage people to reflect on their role in this life in two ways: the micro and the macro. Looking through the micro lens, what is your role as a friend, romantic partner, son or daughter, sibling, parent, leader, co-worker, neighbor, and member of humanity? When there is chaos, how do you usually contribute to the situation? Do you bring drama, mediation, peace, alternative perspectives, hate, compassion, or all the above? It's ok to have experienced all these roles. In fact, I think it's a natural part of the human experience to play different roles in order to widen our depth of knowledge.

The more we experience, the more we learn. For example, when we agree to play the role of the aggressor, we tend to innerstand why others act in similar ways because we have been there and have done similar things. When there is a role reversal, we are on the receiving end of the aggressor and we don't like the way it feels, it makes us appreciate people who are kinder and more considerate. Those lessons can potentially humble us as a species and help teach us how to grow and use our emotions as guiding points instead of limiting our ability to reason. Our emotions can work with us or against us. If we allow our emotions to flow through us as we navigate challenges, they can assist us profoundly. For example, if we experience extreme fear during a situation, it can be an alarm system that can be valuable in the future. If we find ourselves in a similar circumstance where we are fearful, it can remind us of what happened the last time, and we will be reminded to make different choices.

Looking through the macro lens, what do you believe your reason for incarnating was? I'm talking big picture. Whether you know exactly the reason or not, if you dive deep into your inner knowing, you can discern a grand theme. Is it *Service to Others* or *Service to Self*? If you believe you are here to help humanity evolve in some way, that's all you need to know for now. It doesn't matter what you have done in your past or all the wrongs you did before you found yourself on the right path. No one should be judging you anyway, and if they do, it's because they are resisting their own healing, and that has nothing to do with you.

The important thing is knowing your presence during one of the most significant eras of this planet's history is to be part of the change. From there, you can live knowing that you are here to be part of the breakdown of 3D and the liberation of the human species. That's pretty exciting! You feel free when you walk away from fear, anxiety, guilt, and shame. That is when you can step into a more neutral, energetic space, and from there, you will be divinely guided to the next step. Many roles are being played in the collective awakening process, from grid workers to guardians of portals and stargates to ambassadors of light, healers, leaders, architects, engineers, innovators, and so much more. You are here for a reason, whether your role is active, passive, or a combination of both. Holding the space for the collective is a big deal; therefore, each and every person is significant and an equal part of the whole.

AWAKENING THE SOUL'S INFINITE POWER

The following is a channeled message for one of my clients in the United States. She carries a profound influence of ancestral healing in this life and is on a journey to regain her power. This message, spoken from her higher self, resonated so strongly that I felt compelled to include it in this book. Its words are profound and relevant to many who are experiencing a similar journey. It is my hope that this message will inspire others who need to hear it.

My beloved, you and I are intertwined. Your mind is filled with countless questions, a natural part of the human experience as we seek to understand the world around us and unravel the driving forces within us. While essential, the mind plays a dominant role in our experience, and the ego can hold us captive when our thoughts descend into the depths of consciousness. As our conscious mind aligns with the third dimension, illusions, and deceit conspire to keep humanity confined to lower levels of consciousness. Yet, within us, the soul radiates with abundant light, carrying infinite codes of knowledge that must pass through the brain to be processed and understood. It's disheartening that only 10 to 15 percent of these light codes are absorbed, leading to disillusionment and misconceptions. This is the psychological warfare many speak of. The purer our thoughts, we are more open to receiving and embodying these enlightening codes. Sadly, many cannot access high-frequency data due to self-imposed barriers stemming from trauma, fear, and shame. The collective consciousness is riddled with tampered vessels, overpowered and corrupted by external influences. Your mother, for various reasons, is one of those affected individuals.

It has been observed that the lack of control has persisted through many generations. This pattern has been inherited and imprinted in your genetic makeup. It is essential to realize that you can transform this ingrained frequency code within your DNA so that it does not continue to impact future generations. We understand this may seem impossible and are here to provide our full support. As previously discussed, the key to this lies in the functioning of the mind. When the soul and mind are in harmony, and the connection between the brain and heart is firm, any 3D cycle can be broken. The brain interprets the heart's vibration, and the body acts as a powerful and cohesive system. Your purpose is to break the cycle, disrupt the pattern, and embark on a new, energetic path; however, this is a journey that only you can undertake. You have surrounded yourself with a beautiful array of angelic beings to guide and support you, although it is essential to note that they can only accompany you on this journey.

As you maintain your inner strength and activate your spirit, you have the power to sever any ties with traits inherited from your mother that signify control, manipulation, imbalance, enslavement, and limitation. You can embody empowerment, truth, harmony, and liberation by embracing your sovereignty. Believe in your authority, integrity, and purpose; all else will naturally fall into place. By taking charge of your mind and freeing yourself from the influence of the 3D realm, you will experience a transformation and embrace your genuine grace.

There is an incredible power within you that words cannot fully describe. As you embrace this power, those not in harmony with your energy will naturally drift away. This is the law of the Universe. Everything will become apparent, and all your lingering questions will dissolve. Wisdom, once obscured by deceit and illusion, will become *readily available. The barriers that seem impossible are no more substantial than a baby on a bed of toilet paper - they cannot withstand the weight and will crumble like brittle blocks. When humanity recognizes its own strength, these barriers will lose their hold, allowing humanity to rise into its true power and embrace genuine sovereignty. You are so close, my dear. We are all part of an angelic choir, unified and free from religious constraints and division. Open your eyes to the truth, not with your physical sight, but through your soul. Love awaits when you release the '3D paradigms,' limiting beliefs, and societal norms that confine you to the third dimension. You are prepared to step into your true power, bringing abundant light and knowledge to humanity. Soar freely, my dear; you are no longer confined.*

KNOWLEDGE IS SOVEREIGNTY

A few years ago, during a family dinner with my husband and children, we decided to play a game where we would each choose one superpower we could acquire. My daughter excitedly shared that she would be able to read people's minds, my husband said he wanted the ability to fly, and my oldest son said he wanted to be able to teleport. When I asked my younger son what he would choose, he thought about it and said, "*Knowledge.*" I asked him what he meant by that, and he said he wanted the ability to know everything. He explained that his superpower would be knowledge, and he would know everything about the universe. After that night, I thought about what he said. It started me down a trajectory of thoughts, and I had an epiphany that knowledge is what the universe is made up of. It's a network of information compiled from experiences stored within the Akashic records.

Every life, every emotion, and every experience are stored within the collective consciousness. *Where does all that information go? And who benefits from it? Does it just sit there in the Akashic records? Does it serve a purpose?* Those are rhetorical questions, of course. I don't think there is one correct answer to these questions. Every soul lives many experiences that contribute to the collective catalog of shared information. I believe we all have access to that information because we are all connected. Imagine a thumb drive where all our data is stored from each lifetime. When we exit each life, our data is transferred to a collective hard drive, also referred to as the Akashic records. Our unique souls have our own thumb drive to add data as we incarnate into more lives. On a micro level, we have our own catalog of personal experiences and wisdom. On a macro level, we have endless shared experiences and knowledge.

I had a client once that was a rock in a previous life. He was on top of a mountain for hundreds of years. His role in that life was to collect data. His consciousness was recording everything that happened, year after year. He connected to the consciousness of the mountain, the birds, the trees, the other rocks, the dirt, the plants, the insects, the sky, the Sun, and everything around him. In fact, I was told in that session that all beings, such as trees, grass, plants, and rocks that can't move themselves, are constantly recording and communicating with the reality around them. If their consciousness is connected to that life form, they gather data and information for the collective. Much like them, we also record information to gather. Over time, all the information of every moment, in all planets, all stars, and in all universes, is combined and stored as knowledge.

This collective wisdom is knowledge, a sacred part of Source creation. It holds old ideas, patterns, evolutionary wisdom, valuable lessons, light codes, and frequencies. As beings of light, we can create new patterns and generate new knowledge and light codes. We are constantly evolving, shifting, and learning. The dark players have rejected the light and turned their allegiance and sovereignty to a vast network of beings that can no longer create. When a soul goes against the collective light source and turns their back on God, they become disconnected from their light source. When that occurs, they are limited to the frequency they are connected to. This is why they need humanity to be in a low vibration with which they are in resonance. Our low vibration keeps them alive and thriving. Our suffering is the loosh that feeds them. They piggyback off our creations because they can't create anything new.

Essentially, the dark players are stuck in their own loop, so they need us to also be within a loop. I believe knowledge is the gateway to freedom. The more we know, the less we are inhibited by dogmatic, manipulative, and inverted truths that challenge our sovereignty. If they can limit our access to valuable information by controlling the education system and teaching us what they want us to know while restricting what we have access to, then they can keep us on a metaphorical leash. That is why they call it *his-story* because it's their version of the truth. Knowledge is power; therefore, education is a privilege. That is why there are areas of the world where children don't have access to education because they are needed as slaves in some capacity. Depending on areas of wealth, public school education varies. There are elite groups of people worldwide who are exposed to a higher level of information, while the rest of the world is limited. Those who can go to college don't realize that they are subjected to another layer of indoctrination and that their prestigious diploma is a pawn of the 3D.

The dark players want to keep our minds occupied with movies, sports, wars, current events, fictional novels, TV shows, social media, partying, drugs, alcohol, political wars, vacations, religion, division, dark agendas, viruses, climate change, reality TV, shootings, pornography, careers, schooling, and financial limitations. They create problems, illnesses, poverty, hierarchies, secret societies, and dark programs, and they prey on the weakness and vulnerability of the masses. They instill fear throughout the collective with predictive programming, MK-Ultra, medical disinformation, false narratives, and strategic agendas. With all these distractions, it isn't easy to formulate new knowledge when everyone is seemingly on autopilot.

As a collective, we are awakening, and through that awakening process, we are breaking down the box of 3D. Many of us are disconnecting from the 3D game, only to realize it is not designed to advance or to win, so the best option is to change our strategy. We do that by making different choices, stepping out of our loops, and seeking knowledge in any way possible. Books hold a lot of valuable information, and many genuinely authentic books that hold sacred knowledge from our ancestors are being kept from us. Many books are available that portray the version of the narrative they want us to believe while hoarding the real books deep within their private libraries.

It is up to us to go within to access the true records of knowledge that I believe we all have access to. The healthier and more balanced we are, our vibration will be higher. That is when we can disconnect from illusions and reconnect to the collective consciousness. Each one of us is the guardian of collective knowledge. We don't need a book to tell us what we already know. We need to unplug from the illusion and stand in our power. The wisdom will flow like beautiful waterfalls when we unite and hold each other up. Knowledge is power. Knowledge is the key to dismantling the 3D grid. The dark players know that, and it's time that humanity does too.

A MESSAGE FROM A
UNIVERSAL TRAVELER

I had a session once with a client from Finland. Upon speaking with him, it became clear that he was truly special. His soul embodied the true essence of Source energy and had traveled throughout the cosmos to guide more primitive species. When I connected to his higher self, it became clear that the message he was giving us was not just for my client but for the collective at large. In the following paragraphs, I share some of his messages regarding humanity.

The third dimension is one of the lowest manifestations of physical form. It's where matter intertwines with physicalities, such as houses, mountains, cars, forests, oceans, and bodies. However, it is a realm with inherent limitations, especially when compared to the higher dimensions like 4D and beyond, which transcend time constraints. My consciousness is connected to all aspects of creation, like everyone else. I am just tuned into it.

I have many names, but not one single name. I am light - energy that can shift and transform. Gravities transmute, expand, and contract as I move. The higher I go in dimensional fields, the less attached I become to the physical world. I embrace lighter and can acknowledge the presence of all light fractals and particles that overlap and supercharge their path defined by intricate choices and thought patterns. The flow is effortless and expansive, and as I ascend in density, I can connect more quickly to all energy pathways, even if I have yet to create or experience them with my consciousness. We all connect - no singular consciousness or fractal of light does not affect the others. Even the fallen light intentionally dropped into lower-density fields to experience lower consciousness thought fields.

The longer you stay in darkness, the harder it is to escape. Darkness has a magnetic pull that constantly reinforces its presence in the quantum energy field of existence. Those who are protective of it become addicted to refueling and powering lower dimensions. The gratification of trickery and power is the fuel that ignites the lower grids, and humanity has become its prey.

There have been instances in the past where a person seeking power loses control when the power develops a consciousness. This consciousness is greedy, always seeking to grow larger until it consumes itself, resulting in catastrophic outcomes. Humanity is currently on the path toward a devastating destiny that will harm the entire universe. However, many soldiers of light have chosen to come to our world to help us transcend fear and lift us out of enslavement by connecting us to our inner light. This light is the most powerful commodity in the universe and cannot be bought, recreated, or stolen. It can only be temporarily hijacked through illusion and manipulation. Unfortunately, most of humanity is unaware of the hidden powers within them and is blindfolded to the truth. But slowly, the blindfolds are coming off, and the illusion is breaking. The soldiers of light are holding space for a grand awakening where an assertive new light will shine through any illusion or suppression that draws its power from the hijacking of humanity's light. This new light will be so intense that it will shine through any firmament or grid that seeks to suppress it.

The light of humanity, which is the essence of our souls, sustains the matrix. Once we recognize our power and influence over the integrity of the 3D grid, those who protect it will be rendered powerless. My purpose is to hold space, shift ley lines, and terraform the damaged energetic grids of outer Earth to create new patterns conducive to a frequency of 5D and beyond. I do not need to have children to fulfill my role. I am an architect and an alchemist. On the other hand, my brother is an operator directly connected to 3D and working to break it down from the inside. He is a Skywalker, shapeshifter, and warrior spirit fully immersed in the war of consciousness. He has placed himself in the void to assist others.

I chose to share this message in my book because many Starseeds are here to do similar work. He chose the path of holding the space and energetically anchoring a higher frequency to the planet. However, his brother chose a different path with more physical obstacles to insert himself directly into the war and infiltrate from the inside. I have omitted the remainder of the message because it held too many details of their lives. I hope this message gives clarity and insight as examples of passive and active roles within the collective and the significance of both.

THE COURAGE TO CHANGE

I believe humanity is going through a deep spiritual reset. The human race has lost connection with the universe for thousands of years. At a soul level, our galactic DNA is cosmic, and we are intrinsically connected to the quantum field of consciousness. In essence, we are an aspect of the cosmos, as the cosmos are an aspect of us. Throughout generations of genetic manipulation and modification, the God code within the human makeup has been suppressed. Unfortunately, I believe the connection has been severely damaged in some ancestral lines. I have seen this within elite family lines and reptilian human hybrids.

Over time, our epigenetics have reflected trauma, limiting beliefs, and limited connectedness to the metaphysical realm. As a result, the human species has shifted into a low vibrational, God-fearing, religiously controlled, dogmatic reality that is controlled by elitist families, reptilians, negative galactic rulers, and AI. Strict parameters have been placed throughout history, resulting in a convoluted free will structure where people have become complacent with their impending trajectory toward dystopia. Through trickery, illusions, fear, and brainwashing, humans are molded from the time they are born to follow the leaders without question. This is reinforced throughout our lives through mainstream media, financial hierarchies, schools, corporate professions, religion, wars, global conflict, division agendas, and a steady stream of poisons and toxins to keep our bodies riddled with dis-ease.

Time is the glue that holds the 3D grid together. With a matrix of time embedded into our holographic reality, we are more likely to follow a structured mainframe that keeps our souls constantly plugged in. Time controls our lives through strict schedules and deadlines. Most of our reality is centered around what time it is, when we need to do something, or how much time we have left. The very notion of time holds us captive to the 3D parameters and anchors us to this dimension. This dimension is coded by thought, fear, dis-ease, and limiting beliefs. If humans are focused on surviving, they will not tap into their creative side. Imagination, passions, and dreams facilitate the process of co-creating a reality beyond our wildest dreams.

If the collective maintained a vibration of *what-ifs* and limitless possibilities, our abilities to manifest would be immeasurable. Instead, we are continuously fed negative affirmations through Voice of God technology as well as other technologies to suppress us and keep us in a fear-based survival mindset. When most of the collective operates from a survival frequency, the co-creating abilities are limited to that frequency. In other words, if people are in fear, they will attract and create more fear.

In my sessions, I have been shown a strategic timeline led by the dark players to accomplish the transhumanism movement by 2030. This is hidden between the lines of sustainable development, eradicating poverty, gender equality, and global partnership for world peace. Behind the scenes, I believe their woke agendas, gender wars, AI technology, and transhumanistic movements are stealing the divinity of the human race. By enticing humanity with technology enhancements that blur the lines between nature and machine, we are testing the boundaries of the God code within us and what sets our species apart from the cosmos. I believe we are a unique species made up of cosmic DNA. Although we have been genetically modified throughout history, our species holds an unclaimed and untouched divine essence.

Scientists and geneticists have tried to recreate our life force energy, for their benefit. They suppress us because they know our life force holds the key to the purity of absolute creation. They have deactivated DNA sequences to lower our frequency and limit our capabilities. At the same time, they attempt to claim our consciousness for themselves. We are the ultimate creators. They have lost the ability to create, so they ride the coattails of our creations while using them to their benefit. In their effort to create a society under complete dystopian control, they require a total takeover of our consciousness with the implantation of AI influence. That begins with dismantling the family structure and targeting our greatest sense of self, our gender. By manipulating the population with hypersexual influence and gender confusion, our foundation crumbles, and we become more susceptible to further programming. With the heavy influence of virtual reality, superheroes, and enhanced capabilities, the next step is to push humanity toward a virtual-based reality.

Humanity's autonomy becomes blended with fake avatars, cloning, and bionic body parts, and ultimately, the human essence dissolves. Every aspect of what makes us human is gradually being pulled away from us, and many people don't see it happening. The race to 2030 has caused agendas to be enhanced and executed to target the youth of this world. Many teens are attracted to these technological advancements and fall victim to the sexy and appealing packaging that it's all surrounded by. The race to steal our divinity and sovereignty is a dangerous and slippery slope.

So why 2030? There are a lot of speculations, and I have received mixed responses. If I had to pull all the explanations I received during my sessions into one main objective, I would say it has to do with the end of a cycle. You see, much like our individual loops, humanity can fall subject to loops or cycles. Humanity has been in the era of darkness, or Pisces, for roughly 2000 years. It is believed that during the Age of Pisces, humanity sought leaders and saviors to guide them through this period. That was a perfect opportunity for the dark players to insert their agendas and false prophecies to hook humanity in. Looking back on our history, we see humans have a deep-rooted need to follow.

People have been programmed to believe they need a savior to guide them throughout their lives because they cannot thrive independently. They have been programmed to think they are sinners, and people will spend their whole lives operating from a place of unworthiness. They believe that to ascend, they must bow down to a greater being. I don't believe in a God like that. I believe God is unconditional in *his* love and support for all life forms. Even those who stray away from the light and dabble in the dark can return to the light if that is their free will's choice. I think we try to humanize God too much. People find comfort in thinking God is a man or a woman. I don't think *he* is either because *he* is not human. God is a frequency of everything in the universe combined. I don't think there is a word in our vocabulary to describe God. The further the dark players can push us away from God, confuse us, and make us fear God, the easier they can win the spiritual war.

As we embark on a new era of Aquarius, the potential is there for humanity to activate the God code and regain sovereignty. I believe we are at a significant junction in our astrological relation to the cosmos, where the timing is optimal for the human race to persevere and triumph over tyranny. That is why an abundance of souls have volunteered to incarnate as humans to assist in the great awakening of the human species. This planned period is well known to our galactic brothers and sisters throughout the multiverse. We have a lot of assistance and a lot of support.

As people continue to awaken all over the globe, the 3D box breaks down, and they lose control little by little. The race to 2030 on both sides holds a prize so big that both are willing to die for it. The dark players will stop at nothing to manipulate humanity to fall into their trap of ultimate control, where they win. Their prize would be the human species, where they gain complete control, and total enslavement follows - at least until the next era or cycle. The other side holds sovereignty and freedom, resulting in humanity's absolute transformation and evolution. The illusion breaks down when humans activate, awaken, and embrace their powers. The ultimate prize is the grand rising of an entire species and the release of the souls tethered to a reality of darkness.

We are in a pivotal period during this process, and I believe we are winning. The validation from my sessions with children gives me the confidence to share this information with you. I know many new Starseeds would not continue to incarnate if we were not at the point of no return. From my perception, humanity is on an upward trajectory and only grows stronger daily. It is the courage that is being ignited within many souls that is triggering waves of change. The courage to change is a choice and a way of life. It takes courage to go against the grain and to stand up against your family, friends, colleagues, and spouses. This spiritual war has undoubtedly divided the masses into two very distinct categories. Those that embrace change and fight for it, and those that resist and succumb to the dark narrative.

The freedom movement is about patience, strategy, resilience, and faith. I suspect that anyone reading this book is on some level of an awakening. A spiritual journey has many layers that require a certain level of faith, which allows them to push through the darkest periods. Many of us have lost family members, life-long friends, romantic relationships, and potentially even credibility within certain circles. The courage to recognize our programming and embark on a journey of self-discovery, healing, transformation, and ultimate sovereignty takes strength and endurance.

I believe the most challenging part about awakening is doing it alone without any support. I am grateful because I have key players in my life, not in quantity, but in quality. I don't have a lot of close friends or even family, but I hold dear to my heart the ones I do have and give thanks to them every day. Sadly, many of my clients do not have a support system and are fighting this battle alone. However, no one is truly alone because we all have an entourage of support in the astral realm. It's hard for people who can't see it to believe they are there. That's why our animal companions are so important because we can see them. We can hug them, love them, and feel their support when we need it most. Many people have had their families, colleagues, and friends turn their back on them and have been called crazy. The good news is a massive shift has occurred due to the bravery of many. The individual awakenings have significantly contributed to the breakdown and dismantling of the 3D grid. We see evidence of this every day. It may not be apparent through mainstream media because the dark players still control that arena to some degree. However, the energy is different. Through the density of illusion and trickery, more and more people are gaining an overwhelming sense of excitement and anticipation. There is a shift in dynamics, and people are reclaiming their divinity. The collective's roots are becoming stronger as communities unite, sharing resources and holding the space for transition.

The word freedom comes from the Old English word *freodom*, meaning a state of emancipation, liberty, and free will. The Latin root of freedom means *"belonging to the people."* It is my interpretation that the God code is activating within the souls that are willing to receive it. Dormant DNA is activating in people that are reaching higher levels of consciousness, where their bodies can receive the light codes. Because of this, the 3D influence and interference are no longer working. As our bodies adjust to higher frequencies, we become more crystalline and more in-tune with our higher self. This has resulted in the inability of the dark players to maintain control. As the collective becomes more multidimensional, their innate gifts are activating, and people recall their purpose and infinite powers. Our bodies are stronger because our spiritual DNA is activating and connecting to the cosmos. Like antennas of light, we are unstoppable. The energy weapons, EMFs, food toxins, chemical warfare, and demonic entities are not affecting us as they once had.

My conclusion from my most objective level of consciousness is that the more we focus on our own healing, knowing, health, intuition, growth, and self-love, the more we can transmute any level of darkness. By stepping into our absolute truth and embracing the light, the dormant codes will activate within us, and we will shine so bright that it will break down the entire structure upon which the 3D grid is built. As we reach our hands out to join with one another, we break down the walls between us and create magnificent bridges of light that connect us to a powerful network of sovereign beings. I can see future generations of children born into a completely different reality, which can only be accomplished by the souls here today. The generations before us have paved the way, and now it is our turn to step up, spread our wings, and command our freedom. Through the grand rising of humanity, the freedom movement sends ripples of change through portals and dimensions throughout space, reaching other universes, and as it expands, it connects to the origin of light and Source creation.

We are not minuscule fractals of light floating in the vast universe with no purpose. We all play an essential role, and every life matters. What happens here in 3D has an impact on the cosmos. I believe we have an abundance of support from our galactic family as they cheer us on in our pursuit of liberation. They offer support, guidance, compassion, and unconditional love, yet they remind us that we are fully capable to win this battle on our own; we just have to believe we can. So, I ask you, do you believe in yourself? If your answer is No, I humbly ask you to search deep within the depths of your soul and make a choice. If you desire freedom, you are in alignment with freedom. If you are in alignment with freedom, on some level it has already occurred. Try to shift your mindset so that even if you don't feel *free*, you attract the energy of freedom to you.

Take the time to heal and follow the steps in this book. Follow the guidance of others you respect until you reach a space where you trust your own knowing. You will get there in your own divine timing. You don't have to prove yourself to anyone, and you certainly don't need to compare yourself to anyone else. This truly is a marathon that includes runners of all types: beginners, intermediate and advanced sprinters. The important thing to recognize is that the finish line is the same for everyone.

If you answered Yes, you are standing in your power, reclaiming your free will, and reactivating your sovereignty. Congratulations! Take a moment to appreciate how far you have come. Remember that we are all works in progress and we never stop growing and learning. Hold the space for those approaching behind you so that you can pass the baton off to others. We will ascend into a new reality of tranquility and everlasting potential so long as we appreciate each other and work together. Our divinity is in our ability to recognize the light in others so that we can shine together. So, let's shine so bright that we blind the dark players -- and we take back control!

To have a Soul Reading with Sherri Divband, please visit:

www.SherriDivband.com

Sherri's YouTube Channel:

https://www.youtube.com/@SherriDivband

Sherri's Instagram page:

https://www.instagram.com/sherri_divband/

Divinely Guided Children Media YouTube page:

https://www.youtube.com/@DivinelyGuidedChildrenMedia

We Need Your Support

The Aramis Creative Learning Center is pioneering a new era of education. We offer virtual classes in three time-zones: American, Australian, and the United Kingdom. We have over 20 mentors worldwide dedicated to supporting children in a positive and uplifting manor. We offer various classes for children, families, and adults.

We are working to secure funding for our first in-person learning center in West Palm Beach, Florida. We aim to open an Aramis Creative Learning Center in all U.S. states and internationally. Community support is vital to our ability to manifest our vision. We are investing in children's future worldwide and need your support.

If you want to donate, please visit our non-profit, The Aramis Collective. Your donations go towards the first physical center and the continuation of our Divinely Guided Children's books and cartoon animation series.

For more information on Aramis Creative Learning Center, please visit:

www.AramisCreativeLearningCenter.com

https://www.instagram.com/aramis_creative_learning_

To donate to our non-profit, please visit:

www.TheAramisCollective.com

New Earth Education

www.AramisCreativeLearning.com

Sherri Divband founded The Aramis Collective, a non-profit organization that supports children's limitless potential. We believe children should be celebrated for their unique gifts and provided the space and opportunities to explore in safe and supportive environments. This can be possible through a variety of avenues. The way our children are educated is paramount in their development. It will shape who they become later in life. The current education system is designed to limit their potential rather than expand it. This is done through rigorous testing, memorization, and competitive-based learning. Children are creative, intelligent, and intuitive by nature. It is their environment that either serves as a catalyst to expand their potential or it can create blockages that limit it. The Aramis Collective intends to provide abundant possibilities to guide children to become empowered, confident, compassionate, kind, and well-adjusted young adults. This is the true catalyst to a future of evolved, balanced, innovative, and highly intuitive adults. The Aramis Collective comprises three critical components: Aramis Creative Learning Center, Sky Universal, and Jordan Media & Publications. This trinity will offer a wide range of support and guidance for new Earth children. We will need community support to transition The Aramis Collective into a worldwide children's resource center with limitless potential.

www.TheAramisCollective.com

Made in United States
Orlando, FL
13 December 2024

55594410R00141